아이가 주인공인 책

아이는 스스로 생각하고 성장합니다.
아이를 존중하고 가능성을 믿을 때
새로운 문제들을 스스로 해결해 나갈 수 있습니다.

〈기적의 학습서〉는 아이가 주인공인 책입니다.
탄탄한 실력을 만드는 체계적인 학습법으로
아이의 공부 자신감을 높여 줍니다.

가능성과 꿈을 응원해 주세요.
아이가 주인공인 분위기를 만들어 주고,
작은 노력과 땀방울에 큰 박수를 보내 주세요.
〈기적의 학습서〉가 자녀 교육에 힘이 되겠습니다.

학습 스케줄

《기적의 초등 영문법》을 시작하기에 앞서 이 책의 학습 계획표를 세워 보세요.
스스로 지킬 수 있는 오늘의 목표량을 정하고 꾸준히 실천해 보세요.
조금씩이더라도 매일매일 공부하는 습관을 만드는 것이 중요합니다.

학습 내용	학습일	학습 내용	학습일
Unit 1 현재진행형	본책 월 일 워크북 월 일	Unit 1 일반동사의 과거형 (규칙 변화)	본책 월 일 워크북 월 일
Unit 2 현재진행형의 부정문과 의문문	본책 월 일 워크북 월 일	Unit 2 일반동사의 과거형 (불규칙 변화)	본책 월 일 워크북 월 일
Chapter 1 실전 테스트	본책 월 일	Unit 3 일반동사 과거형의 부정문, 의문문	본책 월 일 워크북 월 일
Unit 1 can	본책 월 일 워크북 월 일	Chapter 4 실전 테스트	본책 월 일
Unit 2 must와 have to	본책 월 일 워크북 월 일	Unit 1 부사의 형태와 쓰임	본책 월 일 워크북 월 일
Unit 3 may와 should	본책 월 일 워크북 월 일	Unit 2 빈도부사	본책 월 일 워크북 월 일
Chapter 2 실전 테스트	본책 월 일	Chapter 5 실전 테스트	본책 월 일
Unit 1 be동사의 과거형	본책 월 일 워크북 월 일	Unit 1 시간의 전치사	본책 월 일 워크북 월 일
Unit 2 be동사 과거형의 부정문과 의문문	본책 월 일 워크북 월 일	Unit 2 위치, 장소의 전치사	본책 월 일 워크북 월 일
Chapter 3 실전 테스트	본책 월 일	Chapter 6 실전 테스트	본책 월 일

기적의 초등 영문법 2

서영조 지음

저자 **서영조**

한국외국어대학교 영어과, 동국대학교 대학원 연극영화과 졸업.
20여 년간 국내 학습자들을 위한 유익한 영어 학습 콘텐츠를 개발·집필해 왔다. 초등학생을 위한 영어부터 성인 영어까지, 대상에 따른 맞춤식 접근으로 목표한 바를 쉽게 얻을 수 있는 학습서를 집필하고 있다. 영어를 처음 공부하는 초등 어린이들에게는 소화하기 쉬운 설명과 난이도로, 성인 학습자들에게는 일상생활에 바로 적용할 수 있는 실용적인 콘텐츠로 수많은 독자들에게 각광을 받고 있다. 또한 전문 번역가로서 영어권 도서들과 부산국제영화제를 비롯한 여러 영화제 출품작들을 번역하고 있기도 하다.
지은 책으로 《디즈니 OST 잉글리시》, 《디즈니 주니어 잉글리시 겨울왕국》, 《거의 모든 행동 표현의 영어》, 《영어 회화의 결정적 단어들》 등이 있다.

기적의 초등 영문법 2

Miracle Series – English Grammar for Elementary Students 2

초판 발행 • 2023년 1월 9일

지은이 • 서영조
발행인 • 이종원
발행처 • 길벗스쿨
출판사 등록일 • 2006년 7월 1일 | **주소** • 서울시 마포구 월드컵로 10길 56(서교동)
대표 전화 • 02)332-0931 | 팩스 • 02) 323-0586
홈페이지 • www.gilbutschool.co.kr | 이메일 • gilbutschool@gilbut.co.kr

기획 및 책임편집 • 김소이(soykim@gilbut.co.kr), 이경희 | **디자인** • 이현숙 | **제작** • 이진혁
영업마케팅 • 김진성, 박선경 | **웹마케팅** • 박달님, 권은나 | **영업관리** • 정경화 | **독자지원** • 윤정아, 최희창

편집진행 및 전산편집 • 기본기획 | **표지삽화** • 박지영 | **본문삽화** • 고무미 | **영문 감수** • Ryan P. Lagace
인쇄 • 교보피앤비 | **제본** • 경문제책 | **녹음** • YR미디어

ISBN 979-11-6406-465-6 64740 (길벗 도서번호 30496)
정가 15,000원

제 품 명 : 기적의 초등 영문법 2
제조사명 : 길벗스쿨
제조국명 : 대한민국
전화번호 : 02-332-0931
주 소 : 서울시 마포구 월드컵로 10길 56 (서교동)
제조년월 : 판권에 별도 표기
사용연령 : **10세 이상**
KC마크는 이 제품이 공통안전기준에 적합하였음을 의미합니다.

머리말

우리 아이들에게 영문법은 왜 어려울까요?

초등학생 대부분이 영문법을 어렵고 지루하게 느낍니다. 이 책을 준비하면서 초등학교 4~6학년 학생들에게 '영문법이 어렵게 느껴지는 이유가 무엇인가요?'라고 질문했습니다. 그러자 한 명도 빠짐없이 모두가 '외워야 할 게 많아서'라고 답했습니다.
구체적으로는 to부정사, 동명사 등 외워야 할 '용어'들이 많고, 동사의 변형에서 '예외 규칙'도 알아야 하며, 명사의 복수형도 규칙 변화와 불규칙 변화까지 모두 외워야 해서 어렵다고 했습니다.
영문법은 쉽게 말해서 '**영**어 **문**장을 만드는 **법**칙'이라 할 수 있습니다. 다양한 문장을 만들기 위해서는 다양한 법칙, 즉 규칙이 필요합니다. 그런데 그 규칙들을 억지로 외우려 하면 힘듭니다. 그렇다고 외우지 않으면 제대로 된 문장을 만들어서 말을 하거나 글을 쓸 수 없겠지요. 그렇다면, 어떻게 해야 영문법 규칙들을 덜 힘들게 외울 수 있을까요?

영문법 규칙을 외우는 효과적인 방법은?

바로 문제 풀이를 통해서입니다. 선생님의 강의를 듣는 것만으로는 문법을 온전히 내 것으로 만들 수 없습니다. 문제를 풀며 문장 규칙을 스스로 생각해 보아야 문법을 제대로 이해할 수 있습니다.
《기적의 초등 영문법》은 바로 그런 방법으로 우리 초등학생들의 영어 고민을 해결해 줍니다. 이 책에서는 같은 유형의 문제를 지루하게 기계적으로 풀어가는 단순 드릴을 시키지 않습니다. 다양한 유형의 문제를 고르게 접하면서 스스로 생각하고 적용하며 문법 규칙들을 자연스럽게 익히도록 합니다.
본책의 3단계 문제, 실전 테스트, 그리고 워크북까지 몇 천 개의 다양한 문제를 푸는 사이에 학생들은 자연스럽게 영문법 규칙을 익히게 될 것입니다. 초등학생이 꼭 알아야 할 필수 영문법부터 중등 영어에 대비하는 영문법까지 문법 항목들을 빠짐없이 문제에 녹여냈고, 학생들 눈높이에 맞춘 그림 문제들을 다수 포함하여 지루하지 않게 공부할 수 있도록 했습니다.

영문법은 바르고 정확한 문장 쓰기를 위해 필요한 것

영문법을 공부하는 가장 큰 목적은 영어의 규칙을 알고 영어를 바르고 정확하게 쓰기 위해서라고 할 수 있습니다. 영어 문장을 이루는 규칙인 문법을 잘 알지 못하면 문장을 제대로 쓸 수 없는 것은 당연합니다. 문법 학습은 그동안 읽고 듣고 접했던 영어를 체계적으로 정리하는 계기이자 영어 쓰기 실력을 키우는 기초가 될 것입니다. 또한 영문법의 개념 이해와 문장 쓰기 연습은 정확성이 요구되는 중학 영어에 대비하기 위해 꼭 필요한 학습입니다.

아무쪼록 《기적의 초등 영문법》이 초등학생 여러분의 영문법 학습에 기적의 경험을 가져다주기를 기원합니다.

2023년 1월
저자 서영조

이 책의 특징

문법 규칙을 알면 바르고 정확한 문장을 쓸 수 있습니다.
문법이 곧 쓰기 실력이 되는 기적의 초등 영문법

《기적의 초등 영문법》은 초등 교육과정의 필수 영문법을 쉽게 소개하고, 다양한 문제를 단계별로 풀면서 영문법 규칙을 자연스럽게 익히도록 하며, 문장 쓰기 문제를 통해 영어 라이팅 실력을 키워주고, 다양한 실용문을 통해 실질적인 문법 활용 능력을 길러주는 것을 목표로 합니다.

• 초등 교육과정의 필수 영문법 완벽 정리

초등 교육과정의 필수 영문법을 빠짐없이 소개하고, 중학 기초 문법까지 포함합니다. 이 책만으로 초등 필수 영문법을 완성하고 중학 영문법에 대비할 수 있습니다.

• 친절한 설명과 도표, 그림으로 영문법을 쉽게 학습

낯선 문법 용어와 규칙을 쉽게 이해할 수 있도록 간결하고 친절하게 설명합니다. 핵심 내용을 도표로 정리하여 문법 규칙이 한눈에 들어오게 했고, 이해를 돕는 그림과 해석이 있어 어렵지 않게 학습할 수 있습니다.

• 개념 확인 → 문법 규칙 적용 → 문장 쓰기까지 3단계 학습

3단계로 이루어진 단계별 문제 풀이를 통해 기초적인 개념 확인에서부터 완전한 문장 쓰기까지 점진적으로 학습합니다. 이러한 학습법은 문법 학습의 실제 목표인 '정확한 문장 쓰기' 능력을 향상시키며 중학 서술형 시험에 대비하는 토대가 됩니다.

• 흥미로운 실용문으로 문법 활용 능력과 사고력 배양

동화, 일기, 일정표, 조리법, 대화문 등 일상생활에서 흔히 접할 수 있는 다양한 실용문을 실었습니다. 흥미로운 주제의 실용문을 완성하며 문법 활용 능력과 쓰기 실력을 향상시킬 수 있습니다.

• 무료 동영상 강의와 워크북 등 부가 학습자료 제공

이 책의 문법 개념을 친절하게 설명하는 무료 동영상 강의를 제공하며, 공부한 내용을 꼼꼼하게 점검해 볼 수 있는 워크북과 온라인 부가 학습자료를 제공합니다.

이 책의 구성과 학습법

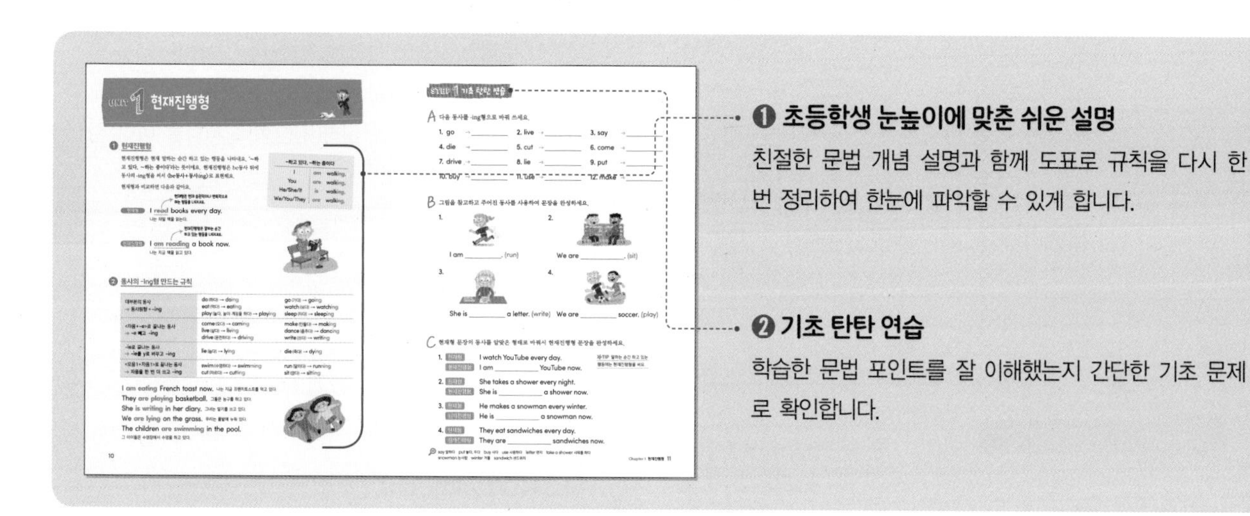

❶ 초등학생 눈높이에 맞춘 쉬운 설명

친절한 문법 개념 설명과 함께 도표로 규칙을 다시 한 번 정리하여 한눈에 파악할 수 있게 합니다.

❷ 기초 탄탄 연습

학습한 문법 포인트를 잘 이해했는지 간단한 기초 문제로 확인합니다.

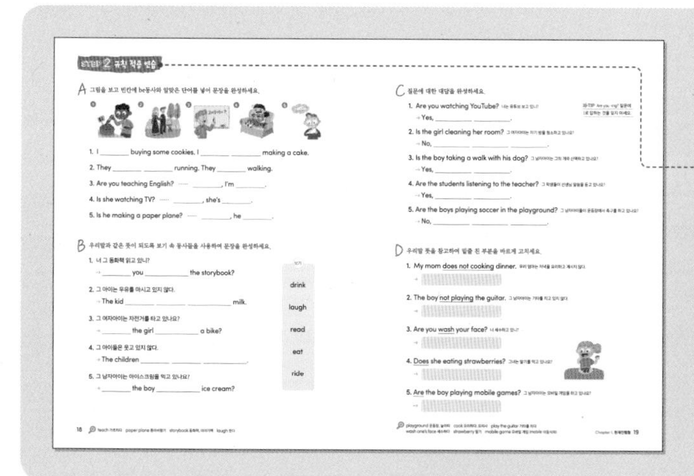

❸ 규칙 적용 연습

배운 문법 규칙을 문장에 적용해 보는 단계입니다. 그림을 보고 고르기, 우리말 뜻에 맞게 빈칸 채우기 등 다양한 유형의 문제를 스스로 생각하며 풀다보면 문법 규칙을 확실히 익힐 수 있습니다.

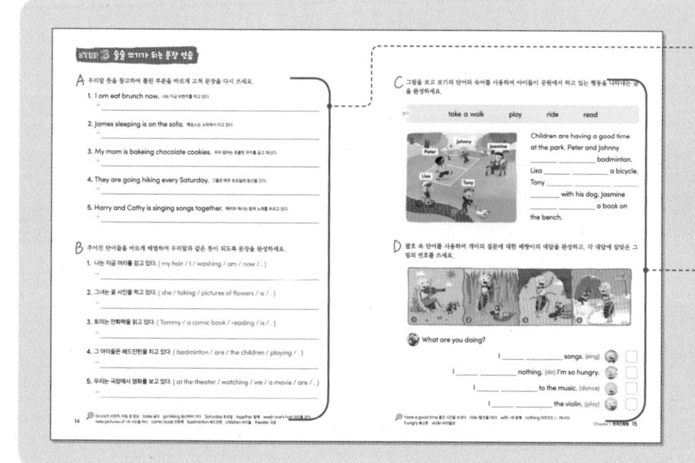

❹ 서술형에 대비하는 문장 쓰기 연습

틀린 곳 찾아 고쳐 쓰기, 바른 순서로 단어 배열하기 등 정확한 규칙과 어순을 연습하며 문장 만들기에 자신감을 키우고 중학 서술형 시험에 대비하는 문장 쓰기를 합니다.

❺ 다양한 실용문 완성하기

일정표, 일기, 조리법, 동화, 대화문 등 다양한 실용문을 문법에 맞게 완성합니다. 문법 규칙을 적용하여 글을 완성해 보면서 실질적인 쓰기 실력을 키울 수 있습니다.

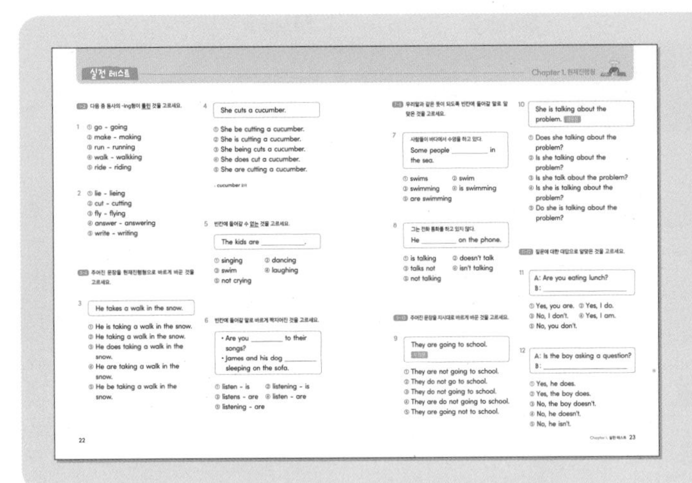

실전 테스트

객관식 문제와 서술형 문제를 통해 각 Chapter에서 학습한 내용을 마지막으로 점검하는 단계입니다. 중학교 내신 시험과 유사하게 구성하여 중학교 시험을 미리 경험하고 대비할 수 있습니다.

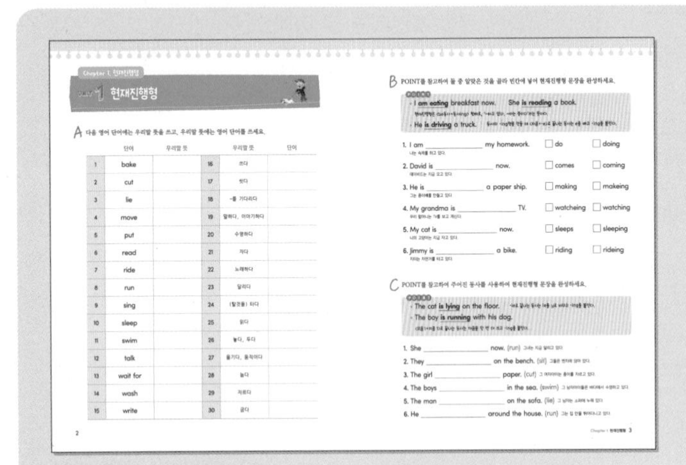

워크북(Workbook)

학습을 마친 후, 워크북의 추가 문제를 풀면서 공부한 내용을 점검하고 복습하며 실력을 다질 수 있습니다. Challenge! 문제는 본책의 전체 문장 쓰기 문제를 업그레이드한 것으로, 학생들의 영어 문장 쓰기 실력을 한 단계 올려줄 것입니다.

부가 학습자료

- Word List (본책 수록)
- 단어 테스트 (워크북 수록)
- 단어 퀴즈 (워크시트 다운로드)
- 문장 받아쓰기 (워크시트 다운로드)

길벗스쿨 e클래스
eclass.gilbut.co.kr

QR코드를 스캔하면 동영상 강의 바로 보기, MP3 파일 및 워크시트 다운로드 등 부가 학습자료를 이용하실 수 있습니다.

무료 동영상 강의

혼자서도 막힘 없이 공부할 수 있도록 무료 동영상 강의를 제공합니다. 문법 개념 설명 부분은 동영상 강의를 보면서 학습하세요.

차례

기적의 초등 영문법 2

기적의 초등 영문법 1

Chapter 1 명사와 관사	Unit 1. 셀 수 있는 명사, 셀 수 없는 명사 Unit 2. 셀 수 있는 명사의 복수형 Unit 3. 관사 a, an, the
Chapter 2 대명사	Unit 1. 인칭대명사의 주격과 목적격 Unit 2. 소유격 인칭대명사와 소유대명사 Unit 3. 비인칭 주어 it Unit 4. 지시대명사 this, that
Chapter 3 be동사의 현재형	Unit 1. be동사의 긍정문과 부정문 Unit 2. be동사의 의문문 Unit 3. There is, There are
Chapter 4 일반동사의 현재형	Unit 1. 일반동사의 긍정문 Unit 2. 일반동사의 부정문 Unit 3. 일반동사의 의문문
Chapter 5 형용사와 수 세기	Unit 1. 형용사의 쓰임과 종류 Unit 2. many, much, a lot of, some, any, a few, a little Unit 3. 셀 수 없는 명사의 수 세기 Unit 4. 기수와 서수

기적의 초등 영문법 3

Chapter 1 미래형	Unit 1. 미래형 긍정문 Unit 2. 미래형 부정문 Unit 3. 미래형 의문문
Chapter 2 의문사	Unit 1. who, what Unit 2. when, where, why Unit 3. how
Chapter 3 비교급, 최상급	Unit 1. 형용사와 부사의 비교급 Unit 2. 형용사와 부사의 최상급
Chapter 4 다양한 문장	Unit 1. 명령문과 제안문 Unit 2. 접속사로 연결되는 문장
Chapter 5 동명사, to부정사	Unit 1. 동명사 Unit 2. to부정사
Chapter 6 문장의 구성 요소	Unit 1. 문장 성분 Unit 2. 품사, 구와 절

CHAPTER 1

현재진행형

동영상 강의

Unit 1. **현재진행형**

Unit 2. **현재진행형의 부정문과 의문문**

현재진행형은 '나는 지금 책을 읽고 있다.', '우리는 밥을 먹는 중이다.'처럼
현재 말하는 순간에 하고 있는 행동을 나타내요. <be동사 + 동사ing>로 표현하는 현재진행형에 대해 배워요.

UNIT 1 현재진행형

❶ 현재진행형

현재진행형은 현재 말하는 순간 하고 있는 행동을 나타내요. '~하고 있다, ~하는 중이다'라는 뜻이에요. 현재진행형은 be동사 뒤에 동사의 -ing형을 써서 〈be동사+동사ing〉로 표현해요.

~하고 있다, ~하는 중이다		
I	am	walking.
You	are	walking.
He/She/It	is	walking.
We/You/They	are	walking.

현재형과 비교하면 다음과 같아요.

현재형은 현재 습관적이나 반복적으로 하는 행동을 나타내요.

현재형 I read books every day.
나는 매일 책을 읽는다.

현재진행형은 말하는 순간 하고 있는 행동을 나타내요.

현재진행형 I am reading a book now.
나는 지금 책을 읽고 있다.

❷ 동사의 -ing형 만드는 규칙

대부분의 동사 → 동사원형 + -ing	do (하다) → doing eat (먹다) → eating play (놀다, 놀이·게임을 하다) → playing	go (가다) → going watch (보다) → watching sleep (자다) → sleeping
<자음+-e>로 끝나는 동사 → -e 빼고 -ing	come (오다) → coming live (살다) → living drive (운전하다) → driving	make (만들다) → making dance (춤추다) → dancing write (쓰다) → writing
-ie로 끝나는 동사 → -ie를 y로 바꾸고 -ing	lie (눕다) → lying	die (죽다) → dying
<모음1+자음1>로 끝나는 동사 → 자음을 한 번 더 쓰고 -ing	swim (수영하다) → swimming cut (자르다) → cutting	run (달리다) → running sit (앉다) → sitting

I am eating French toast now. 나는 지금 프렌치토스트를 먹고 있다.
They are playing basketball. 그들은 농구를 하고 있다.
She is writing in her diary. 그녀는 일기를 쓰고 있다.
We are lying on the grass. 우리는 풀밭에 누워 있다.
The children are swimming in the pool.
그 아이들은 수영장에서 수영을 하고 있다.

STEP 1 기초 탄탄 연습

A 다음 동사를 -ing형으로 바꿔 쓰세요.

1. go → ____________ 2. live → ____________ 3. say → ____________
4. die → ____________ 5. cut → ____________ 6. come → ____________
7. drive → ____________ 8. lie → ____________ 9. put → ____________
10. buy → ____________ 11. use → ____________ 12. make → ____________

B 그림을 참고하고 주어진 동사를 사용하여 문장을 완성하세요.

1.

I am ____________. (run)

2.

We are ____________. (sit)

3.

She is ____________ a letter. (write)

4.

We are ____________ soccer. (play)

C 현재형 문장의 동사를 알맞은 형태로 바꿔서 현재진행형 문장을 완성하세요.

> TIP 말하는 순간 하고 있는 행동에는 현재진행형을 써요.

1. 현재형 I watch YouTube every day.
   현재진행형 I am ____________ YouTube now.

2. 현재형 She takes a shower every night.
   현재진행형 She is ____________ a shower now.

3. 현재형 He makes a snowman every winter.
   현재진행형 He is ____________ a snowman now.

4. 현재형 They eat sandwiches every day.
   현재진행형 They are ____________ sandwiches now.

say 말하다 put 놓다, 두다 buy 사다 use 사용하다 letter 편지 take a shower 샤워를 하다
snowman 눈사람 winter 겨울 sandwich 샌드위치

STEP 2 규칙 적용 연습

A 그림을 보고 보기의 동사들 중 알맞은 것을 사용하여 현재진행형 문장을 완성하세요.

보기 make talk write dance swim

❶ ❷ ❸ ❹ ❺

1. The boy ________ ____________.

2. They ________ ____________.

3. The girl ________ ____________ on the phone.

4. The man ________ ____________ a pizza.

5. The writer ________ ____________ a novel.

B 빈칸을 채워서 현재형 문장을 현재진행형 문장으로 바꾸세요.

1. My dad drives a small car. 우리 아빠는 작은 차를 운전하신다.

   현재진행형 My dad ________ ____________ a small car now.

2. I drink soymilk. 나는 두유를 마신다.

   현재진행형 I ________ ____________ soymilk now.

3. The students eat lunch. 그 학생들은 점심을 먹는다.

   현재진행형 The students ________ ____________ lunch now.

4. The horses run fast. 말은 빨리 달린다.

   현재진행형 The horses ________ ____________ fast now.

5. Mina rides a bike. 미나는 자전거를 탄다.

   현재진행형 Mina ________ ____________ a bike now.

talk 말하다, 이야기하다 phone 전화(기) writer 작가 novel 소설 small 작은 soymilk 두유 fast 빨리 ride a bike 자전거를 타다

C 우리말과 같은 뜻이 되도록 현재형과 현재진행형 중 알맞은 것을 고르세요.

TIP
- **현재형**: 현재 습관적이나 반복적으로 하는 행동
- **현재진행형**: 말하는 순간 하고 있는 행동

1. 나의 언니는 지금 노래하고 있다.
→ My sister (sings / is singing) now.

2. 나는 매일 아침 8시에 학교에 간다.
→ I (go / am going) to school at 8 every morning.

3. 그는 주말마다 영화를 보러 간다.
→ He (goes / is going) to the movies every weekend.

4. 우리는 공원에서 그림을 그리고 있다.
→ We (draw / are drawing) pictures at the park.

5. 그들은 해변에서 산책을 하고 있다.
→ They (take / are taking) a walk on the beach.

D 우리말 뜻에 맞도록 보기의 동사 중 알맞은 것을 사용하여 현재진행형 문장을 완성하세요.

보기	study	brush	wait	look	move	clean

1. John ________ ____________ for Annie. 존은 애니를 기다리고 있다.

2. I ________ ____________ my room now. 나는 지금 내 방을 청소하고 있다.

3. The students ________ ____________ math. 그 학생들은 수학을 공부하고 있다.

4. They ________ ____________ out the window. 그들은 창밖을 내다보고 있다.

5. We ________ ____________ the boxes. 우리는 상자들을 옮기고 있다.

6. The little girl ________ ____________ her teeth. 그 어린 여자아이는 양치질을 하고 있다.

sing 노래하다 go to the movies 영화를 보러 가다 weekend 주말 draw (선으로 그림을) 그리다 park 공원
take a walk 산책하다 beach 해변 move 옮기다, 움직이다 clean 청소하다 wait for ~를 기다리다 room 방
math 수학 look out the window 창밖을 내다보다 little 어린, 작은 brush one's teeth 양치질을 하다

STEP 3 술술 쓰기가 되는 문장 연습

A 우리말 뜻을 참고하여 틀린 부분을 바르게 고쳐 문장을 다시 쓰세요.

1. I am eat brunch now. 나는 지금 브런치를 먹고 있다.
   →

2. James sleeping is on the sofa. 제임스는 소파에서 자고 있다.
   →

3. My mom is bakeing chocolate cookies. 우리 엄마는 초콜릿 쿠키를 굽고 계신다.
   →

4. They are going hiking every Saturday. 그들은 매주 토요일에 등산을 간다.
   →

5. Harry and Cathy is singing songs together. 해리와 캐시는 함께 노래를 부르고 있다.
   →

B 주어진 단어들을 바르게 배열하여 우리말과 같은 뜻이 되도록 문장을 완성하세요.

1. 나는 지금 머리를 감고 있다. (my hair / I / washing / am / now / .)
   →

2. 그녀는 꽃 사진을 찍고 있다. (she / taking / pictures of flowers / is / .)
   →

3. 토미는 만화책을 읽고 있다. (Tommy / a comic book / reading / is / .)
   →

4. 그 아이들은 배드민턴을 치고 있다. (badminton / are / the children / playing / .)
   →

5. 우리는 극장에서 영화를 보고 있다. (at the theater / watching / we / a movie / are / .)
   →

brunch 브런치, 아침 겸 점심 bake 굽다 go hiking 등산하러 가다 Saturday 토요일 together 함께 wash one's hair 머리를 감다 take pictures of ~의 사진을 찍다 comic book 만화책 badminton 배드민턴 children 아이들 theater 극장

C 그림을 보고 보기의 단어와 숙어를 사용하여 아이들이 공원에서 하고 있는 행동을 나타내는 글을 완성하세요.

보기 take a walk　　play　　ride　　read

Children are having a good time at the park. Peter and Johnny ________ ____________ badminton. Lisa ________ ____________ a bicycle. Tony ________ ____________ ________ ________ with his dog. Jasmine ________ ____________ a book on the bench.

D 괄호 속 단어를 사용하여 개미의 질문에 대한 베짱이의 대답을 완성하고, 각 대답에 알맞은 그림의 번호를 쓰세요.

What are you doing?

I ______ __________ songs. (sing) [ ]

I ______ __________ nothing. (do) I'm so hungry. [ ]

I ______ __________ to the music. (dance) [ ]

I ______ __________ the violin. (play) [ ]

have a good time 좋은 시간을 보내다　ride (탈것을) 타다　with ~와 함께　nothing 아무것도 (··· 아니다)
hungry 배고픈　violin 바이올린

현재진행형의 부정문과 의문문

① 현재진행형의 부정문

현재진행형의 부정문은 be동사 뒤에 not을 써요.
〈be동사+not+동사ing〉로 쓰면 되고, '~하고 있지 않다'라는 뜻이 돼요.

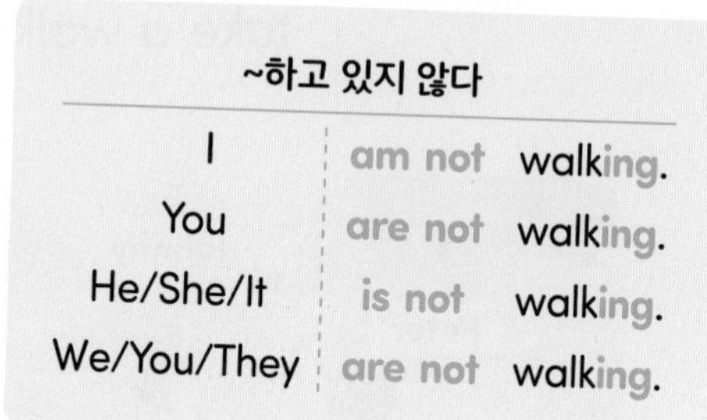

~하고 있지 않다		
I	am not	walking.
You	are not	walking.
He/She/It	is not	walking.
We/You/They	are not	walking.

I am not sleeping. 나는 자고 있지 않다.

You are not talking about it. 너는 그 이야기를 하고 있지 않다.

She is not watering the plants. 그녀는 식물에 물을 주고 있지 않다.

My cousin is not playing with the toys. 나의 사촌은 장난감을 갖고 놀고 있지 않다.

They are not dancing on the stage. 그들은 무대에서 춤을 추고 있지 않다.

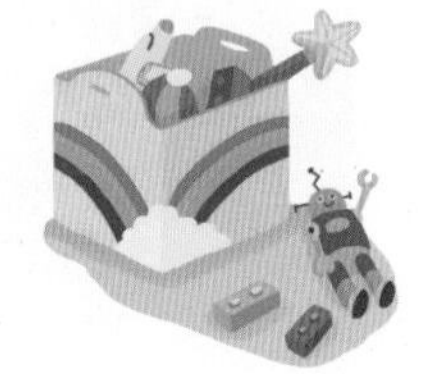

② 현재진행형의 의문문

'~하고 있어요?, ~하는 중이에요?'라고, 말하는 순간 어떤 행동을 하고 있는지 물을 수 있어요. 그런 현재진행형의 의문문은 be동사를 문장 맨 앞으로 보내서 〈be동사+주어+동사ing ~?〉로 써요. 이에 대한 대답은 긍정이면 Yes, 부정이면 No로 해요.

~하고 있나요?	긍정 네, 그래요.	부정 아니요, 그렇지 않아요.
Am I -ing?	Yes, you are.	No, you are not.
Are you -ing?	Yes, I am.	No, I am not.
Is he/she/it -ing?	Yes, he/she/it is.	No, he/she/it is not.
Are we/you/they -ing?	Yes, you/we/they are.	No, you/we/they are not.

Are you reading a book? → 긍정 Yes, I am. 부정 No, I'm not.
너 책 읽고 있니?

Is it raining outside? → 긍정 Yes, it is. 부정 No, it's not. / No, it isn't.
밖에 비가 오고 있나요?

Are they playing the piano? → 긍정 Yes, they are. 부정 No, they're not. / No, they aren't.
그들이 피아노를 치고 있나요?

STEP 1 기초 탄탄 연습

A 각 문장을 부정문으로 바꿀 때 not이 들어갈 자리를 골라 동그라미 하세요.

1. I ① am ② doing ③ my ④ homework. 나는 숙제를 하고 있다.
2. The dogs ① are ② lying ③ on ④ the floor. 그 개들은 바닥에 누워 있다.
3. They ① are ② cleaning ③ the ④ classroom. 그들은 교실을 청소하고 있다.
4. The boy ① and his brother ② are ③ going ④ to school.
   그 남자아이와 그의 형은 학교에 가고 있다.

B 각 문장을 의문문으로 바르게 바꾼 문장에 √ 표시 하세요.

1. I am listening to him.
   나는 그의 말을 귀 기울여 듣고 있다.
   - ☐ Do I listening to him?
   - ☐ Am I listening to him?
2. The baby is crying.
   그 아기는 울고 있다.
   - ☐ Is the baby crying?
   - ☐ Does the baby crying?
3. The cheetahs are running.
   치타들이 달리고 있다.
   - ☐ Is the cheetahs running?
   - ☐ Are the cheetahs running?

C 그림을 보고 괄호 안에서 알맞은 것을 고르세요.

1.

She (is / is not) watching TV.

2.

I (am / am not) sleeping.

3.

A: Are you making sandwiches?
B: (Yes, I am. / No, I'm not.)

4.

A: Is she talking on the phone?
B: (Yes, she is. / No, she isn't.)

do one's homework 숙제를 하다 floor 바닥 classroom 교실 listen (귀 기울여) 듣다 cheetah 치타

STEP 2 규칙 적용 연습

A 그림을 보고 빈칸에 be동사와 알맞은 단어를 넣어 문장을 완성하세요.

❶ ❷ ❸ ❹ ❺

1. I ________ buying some cookies. I ________ ________ making a cake.
2. They ________ ________ running. They ________ walking.
3. Are you teaching English? ----- ________, I'm ________.
4. Is she watching TV? ----- ________, she's ________.
5. Is he making a paper plane? ----- ________, he ________.

B 우리말과 같은 뜻이 되도록 보기 속 동사들을 사용하여 문장을 완성하세요.

보기

drink / laugh / read / eat / ride

1. 너 그 동화책 읽고 있니?
   → ________ you ____________ the storybook?
2. 그 아이는 우유를 마시고 있지 않다.
   → The kid ________ ________ ____________ milk.
3. 그 여자아이는 자전거를 타고 있나요?
   → ________ the girl ____________ a bike?
4. 그 아이들은 웃고 있지 않다.
   → The children ________ ________ ____________.
5. 그 남자아이는 아이스크림을 먹고 있나요?
   → ________ the boy ____________ ice cream?

 teach 가르치다 paper plane 종이비행기 storybook 동화책, 이야기책 laugh 웃다

C 질문에 대한 대답을 완성하세요.

> TIP Are you -ing? 질문에 I로 답하는 것을 잊지 마세요.

1. Are you watching YouTube? 너는 유튜브 보고 있니?
   → Yes, ________ ________.
2. Is the girl cleaning her room? 그 여자아이는 자기 방을 청소하고 있나요?
   → No, ________ ________ ________.
3. Is the boy taking a walk with his dog? 그 남자아이는 그의 개와 산책하고 있나요?
   → Yes, ________ ________.
4. Are the students listening to the teacher? 그 학생들이 선생님 말씀을 듣고 있나요?
   → Yes, ________ ________.
5. Are the boys playing soccer in the playground? 그 남자아이들이 운동장에서 축구를 하고 있나요?
   → No, ________ ________ ________.

D 우리말 뜻을 참고하여 밑줄 친 부분을 바르게 고치세요.

1. My mom does not cooking dinner. 우리 엄마는 저녁을 요리하고 계시지 않다.
   →
2. The boy not playing the guitar. 그 남자아이는 기타를 치고 있지 않다.
   →
3. Are you wash your face? 너 세수하고 있니?
   →
4. Does she eating strawberries? 그녀는 딸기를 먹고 있나요?
   →
5. Are the boy playing mobile games? 그 남자아이는 모바일 게임을 하고 있나요?
   →

playground 운동장, 놀이터 cook 요리하다; 요리사 play the guitar 기타를 치다
wash one's face 세수하다 strawberry 딸기 mobile game 모바일 게임 (mobile 이동식의)

STEP 3 술술 쓰기가 되는 문장 연습

A 각 문장을 지시대로 다시 쓰세요.

1. The boy is running on the track. 그 남자아이는 경주로에서 달리고 있다.

   부정문 ______________________________

2. They are talking about the movie. 그들은 그 영화에 대해 이야기하고 있다.

   부정문 ______________________________

3. You are studying math. 너는 수학을 공부하고 있다.

   의문문 ______________________________

4. She is walking in the rain. 그녀는 빗속을 걷고 있다.

   의문문 ______________________________

5. We are playing the violin in the classroom. 우리는 교실에서 바이올린을 연주하고 있다.

   부정문 ______________________________

B 주어진 단어들을 바르게 배열하여 우리말과 같은 뜻이 되도록 문장을 완성하세요.

1. 나는 도서관에 가고 있지 않다. (not / to the library / I / going / am / .)

   → ______________________________

2. 우리는 TV를 보고 있지 않다. (are / watching TV / we / not / .)

   → ______________________________

3. 민수는 수영장에서 수영을 하고 있지 않다. (Minsu / not / swimming / is / in the pool / .)

   → ______________________________

4. 너는 중국어를 배우고 있니? (you / are / learning / Chinese / ?)

   → ______________________________

5. 그녀는 웹툰을 읽고 있나요? (she / a webtoon / is / reading / ?)

   → ______________________________

track 경주로, 트랙 about ~에 대하여 library 도서관 pool 수영장 learn 배우다 Chinese 중국어 webtoon 웹툰

C 네 사람이 각자 집에서 시간을 보내고 있어요. 보기 속 동사들을 사용하여 현재진행형 부정문으로 글을 완성하세요. (동사는 한 번씩만 쓰세요.)

보기

run
clean
read
wash

Harry is running on a treadmill. He ________ ________ ____________ on the street. Brad is watching TV. He ________ ________ ____________ a book. Annie is cooking dinner. She ________ ________ ____________ the dishes. Julia is doing yoga. She ________ ________ ____________ the house.

D 에마와 친구가 통화하고 있어요. 주어진 동사들을 사용하여 현재진행형으로 대화를 완성하세요.

A: Hi, Emma. What ______ you __________? (do)

B: I'm home. I ______ __________ on the sofa and __________ TV. (sit, watch) My dog Coco ______ __________ beside me. (sleep) How about you?

A: I'm with Amy. We ______ __________ bicycles at the park. (ride) Come and play with us.

B: Okay.

treadmill 러닝머신 street 거리 wash the dishes 설거지를 하다 yoga 요가 beside ~ 옆에

실전 테스트

1-2 다음 중 동사의 -ing형이 틀린 것을 고르세요.

1 ① go - going
② make - making
③ run - running
④ walk - walkking
⑤ ride - riding

2 ① lie - lieing
② cut - cutting
③ fly - flying
④ answer - answering
⑤ write - writing

3-4 주어진 문장을 현재진행형으로 바르게 바꾼 것을 고르세요.

3

He takes a walk in the snow.

① He is taking a walk in the snow.
② He taking a walk in the snow.
③ He does taking a walk in the snow.
④ He are taking a walk in the snow.
⑤ He be taking a walk in the snow.

4

She cuts a cucumber.

① She be cutting a cucumber.
② She is cutting a cucumber.
③ She being cuts a cucumber.
④ She does cut a cucumber.
⑤ She are cutting a cucumber.

* cucumber 오이

5 빈칸에 들어갈 수 없는 것을 고르세요.

The kids are ____________.

① singing ② dancing
③ swim ④ laughing
⑤ not crying

6 빈칸에 들어갈 말로 바르게 짝지어진 것을 고르세요.

• Are you ____________ to their songs?
• James and his dog ____________ sleeping on the sofa.

① listen - is ② listening - is
③ listens - are ④ listen - are
⑤ listening - are

7-8 우리말과 같은 뜻이 되도록 빈칸에 들어갈 말로 알맞은 것을 고르세요.

7

사람들이 바다에서 수영을 하고 있다.

Some people __________ in the sea.

① swims ② swim
③ swimming ④ is swimming
⑤ are swimming

8

그는 전화 통화를 하고 있지 않다.

He __________ on the phone.

① is talking ② doesn't talk
③ talks not ④ isn't talking
⑤ not talking

9-10 주어진 문장을 지시대로 바르게 바꾼 것을 고르세요.

9

They are going to school. 부정문

① They are not going to school.
② They do not go to school.
③ They do not going to school.
④ They are do not going to school.
⑤ They are going not to school.

10

She is talking about the problem. 의문문

① Does she talking about the problem?
② Is she talking about the problem?
③ Is she talk about the problem?
④ Is she is talking about the problem?
⑤ Do she is talking about the problem?

11-12 질문에 대한 대답으로 알맞은 것을 고르세요.

11

A: Are you eating lunch?
B: ____________________

① Yes, you are. ② Yes, I do.
③ No, I don't. ④ Yes, I am.
⑤ No, you don't.

12

A: Is the boy asking a question?
B: ____________________

① Yes, he does.
② Yes, the boy does.
③ No, the boy doesn't.
④ No, he doesn't.
⑤ No, he isn't.

13-14 다음 중 우리말을 영어로 바르게 옮긴 것을 고르세요.

13

그들은 그네를 타고 있지 않다.

① They are playing on the swings.
② They do not playing on the swings.
③ They are not playing on the swings.
④ They are playing not on the swings.
⑤ They are do not playing on the swings.

* swings 그네

14

그들은 거리를 청소하고 있나요?

① Do they cleaning the street?
② Are they clean the street?
③ Does they cleans the street?
④ Are they cleaning the street?
⑤ Do they are cleaning the street?

15 다음 중 올바른 문장을 고르세요.

① I am eat eggs every day.
② The boys isn't playing soccer.
③ She is drinks coffee with her husband.
④ The man are driving a bus.
⑤ They are watching TV together.

* husband 남편

16 빈칸에 들어갈 말이 나머지와 다른 하나를 고르세요.

① The cat ______ lying on the bed.
② ______ the boy having lunch?
③ The kids ______ swimming.
④ My mom ______ cleaning the house.
⑤ He ______ not taking a shower.

17 다음 문장을 바르게 고치는 방법으로 알맞은 것을 고르세요.

Do the girls having lunch now?

① having을 has로 고친다.
② Do를 Are로 고친다.
③ Do를 Does로 고친다.
④ lunch를 a lunch로 고친다.
⑤ having을 are having으로 고친다.

18 빈칸에 공통으로 들어갈 말을 쓰세요.

- John and Emily ________ reading books.
- They ________ not eating cookies now.

19-20 우리말 뜻에 맞도록 틀린 부분을 바르게 고쳐 문장을 다시 쓰세요.

19

It does raining outside.

밖에 비가 오고 있다.

→ ____________________

* outside 밖에

20

My mom isn't cooking dinner every day.

우리 엄마는 저녁을 매일 요리하지는 않으신다.

→ ____________________

21 우리말과 같은 뜻이 되도록 빈칸에 알맞은 말을 써 넣어 대화를 완성하세요.

A: 그 학생들은 지금 그림을 그리고 있나요?
________ the students ________ pictures now?

B: 아니요.
No, ________ ________.

22 질문에 대한 대답을 완성하세요.

A: Are the boys playing with the cats?

B: Yes, ________ ________.

23 주어진 단어들을 바르게 배열하여 우리말과 같은 뜻이 되도록 문장을 완성하세요.

나는 지하철을 기다리고 있다.

(the subway / I / waiting for / am / .)

→ ____________________

____

* subway 지하철

24-25 주어진 단어들을 사용하여 우리말과 같은 뜻의 영어 문장을 쓰세요.

24

그는 숙제를 하고 있지 않다.

(do, his homework)

→ ____________________

25

너는 음악 듣고 있니? (listen to, music)

→ ____________________

Word List Chapter 1

앞에서 배운 단어를 한 번 더 확인하고 어렵거나 모르는 단어는 다시 공부하세요.

☐ bake	굽다	☐ beach	해변
☐ buy	사다	☐ clean	청소하다
☐ cut	자르다	☐ draw	(선으로 그림을) 그리다
☐ drive	운전하다	☐ floor	바닥
☐ hungry	배고픈	☐ laugh	웃다
☐ learn	배우다	☐ letter	편지
☐ library	도서관	☐ lie	눕다
☐ listen	(귀 기울여) 듣다	☐ live	살다
☐ make	만들다	☐ math	수학
☐ move	옮기다	☐ nothing	아무것도 (… 아니다)
☐ novel	소설	☐ put	놓다, 두다
☐ ride	(탈것을) 타다	☐ say	말하다
☐ sing	노래하다	☐ sleep	자다
☐ strawberry	딸기	☐ street	거리
☐ swim	수영하다	☐ talk	말하다, 이야기하다
☐ teach	가르치다	☐ together	함께
☐ use	사용하다	☐ wait for	~를 기다리다
☐ weekend	주말	☐ write	쓰다

CHAPTER 2

조동사

동영상 강의

조동사는 동사 앞에 쓰여서 동사에 다른 뜻을 더해주는 역할을 해요.
'~할 수 있다', '~해야 한다', '~해도 된다', '~하는 게 좋다'라는 의미의 조동사를 배워요.

UNIT 1 can

① 조동사 can

조동사 can은 '**~할 수 있다**'라는 뜻을 나타내요.
조동사이므로 뒤에는 동사의 원래 형태인 동사원형이 와요.

I **can play** the piano. 나는 피아노를 칠 수 있다.

She **can swim**. 그녀는 수영할 수 있다.

They **can speak** English. 그들은 영어를 할 수 있다.

조동사는 동사 앞에 쓰여서 동사에 '할 수 있다, 해야 한다, 해도 된다' 같은 뜻을 더해주는 역할을 해요.
조동사에는 can, may, must, should 등이 있어요.
조동사 뒤에는 항상 동사의 원래 형태인 동사원형이 와요.

② can의 부정문

'**~할 수 없다**'라는 부정의 의미는 ⟨**cannot+동사원형**⟩으로 나타내요. cannot은 보통 줄여서 can't로 써요.

I **cannot cook**. 나는 요리를 하지 못한다.

She **can't dance**. 그녀는 춤을 추지 못한다.

We **can't play** soccer on rainy days.
우리는 비 오는 날에는 축구를 할 수 없다.

can + 동사원형	~할 수 있다
cannot [can't] + 동사원형	~할 수 없다, ~하지 못한다

③ can의 의문문

'**~할 수 있어요?**'라고 물어보는 의문문은 조동사 can을 주어 앞에 보내서 ⟨**Can+주어+동사원형 ~?**⟩으로 써요.
이때 긍정 대답은 Yes로, 부정 대답은 No로 해요.

Can you **swim**? 너 수영할 수 있어?

Can he **speak** English? 그는 영어를 할 수 있어요?

~할 수 있어요?	긍정 네, 할 수 있어요.	부정 아니요, 할 수 없어요.
Can you ride a bike? 너 자전거 탈 수 있어?	Yes, I can. 응, 탈 수 있어.	No, I can't. 아니, 못 타.
Can she cook rice? 그녀는 밥을 할 수 있어요?	Yes, she can. 네, 할 수 있어요.	No, she can't. 아니요, 못 해요.
Can they play tennis? 그들은 테니스를 칠 수 있어요?	Yes, they can. 네, 칠 수 있어요.	No, they can't. 아니요, 못 쳐요.

STEP 1 기초 탄탄 연습

A 그림을 참고하여 올바른 문장에 √ 표시 하세요.

TIP 조동사는 동사 앞에 오고, 조동사의 부정문은 조동사 뒤에 not을 써요. 조동사의 의문문은 조동사를 주어 앞으로 보내요.

1. ☐ I read can English.
   ☐ I can read English.

2. ☐ She can't run fast.
   ☐ She can run not fast.

3. ☐ Can you bake cookies?
   ☐ Can bake you cookies?

B 그림을 보고 괄호 안에서 알맞은 것을 고르세요.

1. I (can / can't) play the guitar.

2. It (can / can't) fly.

3. They (can / can't) play baseball.

4. 你吃饭没?
???
John (can / can't) speak Chinese.

C 질문에 대한 대답으로 알맞은 것에 √ 표시 하세요.

1. Can you swim? ☐ Yes, I do. ☐ Yes, I can.
2. Can she sing the song? ☐ Yes, she can. ☐ No, she can.
3. Can he ride a bike? ☐ Yes, he can't. ☐ No, he can't.
4. Can the boys play basketball? ☐ Yes, they can. ☐ No, they don't.

baseball 야구 basketball 농구

STEP 2 규칙 적용 연습

A 그림을 보고 can, can't 중 알맞은 것과 주어진 동사를 사용하여 문장을 완성하세요.

❶ ❷ ❸ ❹ ❺

I am going to tell you...

ski　speak　fix　pass　jump

1. The girl ____________ ____________.
2. He ____________ ____________ English.
3. They ____________ ____________ the toy car.
4. The student ____________ ____________ the test.
5. The frog ____________ ____________ high.

B 우리말과 같은 뜻이 되도록 주어진 동사와 조동사를 사용하여 문장을 완성하세요.

1. 나는 내일 그 파티에 갈 수 있다. (go)
   → ________ ________ ________ to the party tomorrow.
2. 너는 그 방에 들어갈 수 없다. (enter)
   → ________ ________ ________ the room.
3. 너 그 문제 풀 수 있니? (solve)
   → ________ ________ ________ the problem?
4. 그녀는 아침에 일찍 일어나지 못한다. (get up)
   → ________ ________ ________ ________ early in the morning.
5. 그들은 새를 그릴 수 있나요? (draw)
   → ________ ________ ________ birds?

ski 스키를 타다　fix 고치다, 수리하다　pass 통과하다　jump 점프하다　test 시험　high 높이; 높은　enter 들어가다　solve 풀다, 해결하다　problem 문제　get up 일어나다　early 일찍

C 질문에 대한 대답을 완성하세요.

1. A: Can you wash the dishes now? 너는 지금 설거지할 수 있니?

   B: Yes, ________ ________.

2. A: Can David come to the concert? 데이비드는 그 음악회에 올 수 있나요?

   B: No, ________ ________.

3. A: Can we sit here? 우리 여기 앉을 수 있나요?

   B: Yes, ________ ________.

TIP you로 물으면 I로 답하고, we로 물으면 상황에 따라 we나 you로 답해요. 남성 단수 명사로 물으면 he로, 여성 단수 명사로 물으면 she로 답해요. 복수 명사로 물으면 they로 답해요.

4. A: Can your grandmother use a computer? 네 할머니는 컴퓨터를 사용하실 수 있니?

   B: Yes, ________ ________.

5. A: Can your parents go there tomorrow? 네 부모님은 내일 거기 가실 수 있니?

   B: No, ________ ________.

D 각 문장을 지시대로 바꿔서 문장을 완성하세요.

1. I can eat vegetables. 나는 채소를 먹을 수 있다.

   부정문 ________________ vegetables.

2. She can swim well. 그녀는 수영을 잘할 수 있다.

   의문문 ________________ well?

3. The old man can walk. 그 노인은 걸을 수 있다.

   부정문 ________________________.

4. You can carry the bag. 너는 그 가방을 들 수 있다.

   의문문 ________________ the bag?

5. The girl can speak French. 그 여자아이는 프랑스어를 할 수 있다.

   의문문 ________________ French?

concert 콘서트, 음악회 here 여기에 grandmother 할머니 parents 부모 there 거기에
vegetable 채소 well 잘 carry 들다, 운반하다 French 프랑스어

STEP 3 술술 쓰기가 되는 문장 연습

A 우리말 뜻을 참고하여 틀린 부분을 바르게 고쳐 문장을 다시 쓰세요.

1. Jin can comes here tonight. 진은 오늘 밤에 여기 올 수 있다.

→ ____________________

2. The man can drive not a car. 그 남자는 운전을 할 수 없다.

→ ____________________

3. Can you reading this English word? 너 이 영어 단어 읽을 수 있니?

→ ____________________

4. We play cannot baseball here. 우리는 여기서 야구를 할 수 없다.

→ ____________________

5. Can the girl eats carrots? 그 여자아이는 당근을 먹을 수 있나요?

→ ____________________

B 주어진 단어들을 바르게 배열하여 우리말과 같은 뜻이 되도록 문장을 완성하세요.

1. 나는 종이배를 만들 수 있다. (make / I / a paper boat / can / .)

→ ____________________

2. 폴은 이 문제를 풀지 못한다. (this problem / Paul / solve / can't / .)

→ ____________________

3. 나 좀 도와줄 수 있어요? (help / can / me / you / ?)

→ ____________________

4. 그들은 한국어를 이해할 수 없다. (they / Korean / understand / can't / .)

→ ____________________

5. 그녀는 커피를 마실 수 있나요? (she / drink / can / coffee / ?)

→ ____________________

tonight 오늘 밤에; 오늘 밤 word 단어 carrot 당근 paper boat 종이배 help 돕다 understand 이해하다 Korean 한국어, 한국인; 한국의

C 지수가 할 수 있는 일과 할 수 없는 일을 나타낸 그림을 보고 can이나 can't와 보기의 동사들을 사용하여 글을 완성하세요.

What Jisu Can Do & Cannot Do

Jisu is 13 years old. She is in the sixth grade of elementary school.

She learns English at school. So she ________ ____________ English. But she ________ ____________ Chinese.

She ________ ____________ a bicycle. But she ________ ____________ a scooter.

She likes to play on the beach. She ________ ____________ a sandcastle. But she ________ ____________.

She likes music. She ________ ____________ the piano. But she ________ ____________ the guitar.

보기

build
speak
play
swim
ride

grade 학년 elementary school 초등학교 so 그래서 scooter 킥보드 build 짓다, 세우다 sandcastle 모래성

UNIT 2 must와 have to

1 조동사 must

'반드시 ~해야 한다'라고 말할 때는 조동사 must를 써요. 조동사이므로 뒤에는 동사원형이 와요.
부정 표현인 〈must not+**동사원형**〉은 **'~하면 안 된다'**라는 뜻이에요.

must + **동사원형**	~해야 한다
must not + **동사원형**	~하면 안 된다

긍정

I **must do** my homework. 나는 숙제를 해야 한다.

You **must clean** your room. 너는 네 방을 청소해야 한다.

He **must get up** at 7. 그는 7시에 일어나야 한다.

부정

You **must not drink** this. 너는 이걸 마시면 안 된다.

She **must not open** the window tonight. 그녀는 오늘 밤 창문을 열면 안 된다.

They **must not play** soccer here. 그들은 여기서 축구를 하면 안 된다.

2 조동사 have to

have to는 must와 같은 뜻이에요. **'~해야 한다'**라는 뜻이죠. 차이가 있다면 have to는 주어가 3인칭 단수일 때는 has to로 써야 한다는 것이에요. have to 뒤에도 동사원형이 와요.
그러나 have to의 부정문은 must의 부정문과 의미가 달라요. 부정문 〈don't/doesn't have to+**동사원형**〉은 **'~할 필요 없다, ~하지 않아도 된다'**라는 뜻이에요.

have to (has to) + **동사원형**	~해야 한다
don't have to (doesn't have to) + **동사원형**	~할 필요 없다, ~하지 않아도 된다

긍정

You **have to take** this train. 너는 이 기차를 타야 한다.

He **has to wear** a school uniform. 그는 교복을 입어야 한다.

Emily **has to wash** her hands. 에밀리는 손을 씻어야 한다.

→ 주어가 3인칭 단수일 때는 have to가 아닌 has to로 써야 해요.

부정

You **don't have to do** it today. 너는 오늘 그걸 하지 않아도 된다.

He **doesn't have to drive** a car. 그는 운전할 필요가 없다.

→ 주어가 3인칭 단수일 때는 doesn't have to로 써요.

We **don't have to borrow** the book. 우리는 그 책을 빌리지 않아도 된다.

STEP 1 기초 탄탄 연습

A 우리말 뜻을 참고하여 괄호 안에서 알맞은 것을 고르세요.

1. I (must / has to) call my mom. 나는 엄마한테 전화해야 한다.
2. We (must / have) to buy a new desk. 우리는 새 책상을 사야 한다.
3. He (has / have) to return the book. 그는 그 책을 돌려줘야 한다.
4. You don't (has / have) to watch it. 너는 그것을 보지 않아도 된다.

B 그림을 보고 괄호 안에서 알맞은 것을 고르세요.

1. 

He (must / must not) get up now.

2. 

I (have to / don't have to) wash the dishes.

3. 

You (must / must not) eat after 9.

4. 

She (has to / doesn't have to) go this way.

C 밑줄 친 부분의 의미로 알맞은 것을 골라 √ 표시 하세요.

1. You must keep your promise. ☐ ~할 필요 없다 ☐ ~해야 한다
2. Violet has to brush her teeth. ☐ ~해야 한다 ☐ ~하지 않아도 된다
3. You must not go home now. ☐ ~하면 안 된다 ☐ ~하지 않아도 된다
4. We don't have to go to school today. ☐ ~하면 안 된다 ☐ ~하지 않아도 된다

call 전화하다 return 돌려주다 after + 시간 ~ 후에 this way 이쪽으로 promise 약속
keep one's promise 약속을 지키다

STEP 2 규칙 적용 연습

A 그림을 보고 have to나 must not 중 알맞은 것을 골라 빈칸에 쓰세요. (필요한 경우 동사의 형태를 바꾸세요.)

❶ ❷ ❸ No! ❹ ❺

1. I ______________________ go there by 9 a.m.

2. You ______________________ swim here.

3. We ______________________ eat too much chocolate or candy.

4. He ______________________ see a doctor.

5. We ______________________ cross the road at a red light.

B 우리말에 맞는 부정문이 되도록 괄호 안에서 알맞은 것을 골라 빈칸에 쓰세요.

1. 너는 밤늦게 노래를 부르면 안 된다. (must not / don't have to)
   → You ______________________ sing late at night.

2. 그녀는 그들을 기다리지 않아도 된다. (must not / doesn't have to)
   → She ______________________ wait for them.

3. 그들은 학교에 늦으면 안 된다. (must not / don't have to)
   → They ______________________ be late for school.

4. 당신은 오늘 저녁 식사를 만들지 않아도 돼요. (must not / don't have to)
   → You ______________________ cook dinner today.

5. 그는 그 편지에 답장을 쓰지 않아도 된다. (must not / doesn't have to)
   → He ______________________ reply to the letter.

by + 시간 ~까지 see a doctor 진찰받다, 병원에 가다 cross 건너다, 횡단하다 road 도로, 길 red light 빨간 신호등 late at night 밤늦게 be late for ~에 늦다 reply to ~에 대답하다, 답장을 보내다

C 그림을 참고하여 알맞은 동사와 괄호 속 조동사를 사용하여 문장을 완성하세요. (필요한 경우 동사의 형태를 바꾸세요.)

take feed brush wear

1. 너는 매일 밤 양치질을 해야 한다. (must)
   → You ______________________ your teeth every night.

2. 그는 마스크를 써야 한다. (have to)
   → He ______________________ a mask.

3. 우리는 여기서 사진을 찍으면 안 된다. (must not)
   → We ______________________ pictures here.

4. 그녀는 그 개에게 먹이를 주지 않아도 된다. (don't have to)
   → She ______________________ the dog.

D 각 영어 문장의 우리말 해석을 완성하세요.

1. I must take the 10 o'clock train.
   → 나는 10시 기차를 ______________________.

2. She has to study for the exam.
   → 그녀는 시험을 위해 ______________________.

3. We don't have to go there today.
   → 우리는 오늘 거기 ______________________.

4. They must not run in the museum.
   → 그들은 박물관에서 ______________________.

feed 먹이를 주다 wear a mask 마스크를 쓰다 take pictures 사진을 찍다 exam 시험
museum 박물관, 미술관

STEP 3 술술 쓰기가 되는 문장 연습

A 우리말 뜻을 참고하여 틀린 부분을 바르게 고쳐 문장을 다시 쓰세요.

1. She must gets up early tomorrow morning. 그녀는 내일 아침에 일찍 일어나야 한다.

→ ______________________________

2. Tommy have to go to school today. 토미는 오늘 학교에 가야 한다.

→ ______________________________

3. I have not to wash my hair today. 나는 오늘은 머리를 안 감아도 된다.

→ ______________________________

4. You don't must drink too much Coke. 너는 콜라를 너무 많이 마시면 안 된다.

→ ______________________________

5. He don't have to take an umbrella today. 그는 오늘 우산을 안 가져가도 된다.

→ ______________________________

B 주어진 단어들을 바르게 배열하여 우리말과 같은 뜻이 되도록 문장을 완성하세요.

1. 우리는 시간을 아껴야 한다. (must / time / save / we / .)

→ ______________________________

2. 그녀는 기차를 타고 그곳에 가야 한다. (by train / she / go there / has to / .)

→ ______________________________

3. 너는 늦게 자면 안 된다. (late / must not / you / go to bed / .)

→ ______________________________

4. 나는 문을 잠그지 않아도 된다. (the door / I / lock / don't have to / .)

→ ______________________________

5. 우리는 매일 운동을 해야 한다. (exercise / we / every day / have to / .)

→ ______________________________

too much 너무 많은 Coke (코카)콜라 umbrella 우산 save 아끼다, 모으다 by train 기차로 lock 잠그다 exercise 운동하다

C 그림을 보고 빈칸에 알맞은 단어를 써서 도서관 이용 규칙을 완성하세요.

1. You ________ ________ a membership card to use the library.
2. You have ________ ________ quiet in the reading room.
3. You ________ ________ ________ food.
4. You ________ ________ ________ in the reading room.
5. You ________ ________ scribble in books.
6. You ________ ________ ________ your pets.
7. You ________ ________ the desks and chairs clean.

rule 규칙 membership card 회원증 quiet 조용한 scribble 낙서하다 bring 데려오다, 가져오다 pet 반려동물 keep ~한 상태로 유지하다 clean 깨끗한 reading room 열람실

UNIT 3 # may와 should

1 조동사 may

조동사 may는 **'~해도 된다'**라는 뜻으로, '허락'을 나타내요.
뒤에는 역시 동사원형이 와요.
부정형 may not은 **'~하면 안 된다'**는 의미이긴 하지만, 앞에서 배운 must not(절대로 ~하면 안 된다)보다는 약하게 금지하는 느낌이에요.

may + 동사원형	~해도 된다
may not + 동사원형	~하면 안 된다 (약하게)

긍정

You **may come** in. 들어와도 돼요.

They **may leave** now. 그들은 지금 떠나도 돼요.

부정

She **may not sit** here. 그녀는 여기에 앉으면 안 돼요.

They **may not play** soccer here. 그들은 여기서 축구를 하면 안 돼요.

2 may의 의문문

'~해도 될까요?'라고 허락을 구하는 의문문은 may를 주어 앞으로 보내서 **〈May+주어+동사원형 ~?〉**으로 써요.
대답은 Yes와 No를 써서 해요.

의문문	
May + 주어 + 동사원형 ~?	~해도 될까요?
대답	
Yes, 주어 + may.	네, 돼요.
No, 주어 + may not.	아니요, 안 돼요.

May I **come** in? 들어가도 될까요?

→ 긍정 **Yes**, you **may**. 네, 들어와도 돼요.

→ 부정 **No**, you **may not**. 아니요, 들어오면 안 돼요.

3 조동사 should

조동사 should는 **'~하는 게 좋다, ~해야 한다'**라는 뜻으로, '충고'나 '조언'을 나타내요.
must나 have to처럼 '~해야 한다'라고 해석하지만 '의무'를 나타내는 그 둘보다는 의미가 좀 약해요.
부정형인 should not은 **'~하지 않는 게 좋다, ~하면 안 된다'**라는 뜻이에요.

should + 동사원형	~하는 게 좋다, ~해야 한다
should not + 동사원형	~하지 않는 게 좋다, ~하면 안 된다

긍정 You **should go** to bed early. 일찍 자는 게 좋아.

부정 You **should not go** to bed late. 늦게 자지 않는 게 좋아.

STEP 1 기초 탄탄 연습

A 올바른 문장에 √ 표시 하세요.

1. ☐ You may drink this. ☐ You may to drink this.
2. ☐ May read I this book? ☐ May I read this book?
3. ☐ We should have breakfast. ☐ We should having breakfast.
4. ☐ You should not watch TV now. ☐ You don't should watch TV now.

B 그림을 보고 괄호 안에서 알맞은 것을 고르세요.

1. You (may / may not) eat this.

2.
She (may / may not) wear her sister's coat.

3. You (should / should not) exercise every day.

4. People (should / should not) walk on the grass.

C 질문에 대한 대답으로 알맞은 것에 √ 표시 하세요.

1. May I sit here? ☐ Yes, I may. ☐ Yes, you may.
2. May Kate use this pen? ☐ Yes, she may. ☐ No, she may.
3. May he come with us? ☐ Yes, he does. ☐ Yes, he may.
4. May I go to your house? ☐ Yes, you do. ☐ No, you may not.

breakfast 아침 식사 coat 외투 grass 잔디밭, 풀밭, 풀

STEP 2 규칙 적용 연습

A 그림을 보고 괄호 안에서 알맞은 표현을 골라 빈칸에 쓰세요.

① ② 

③ 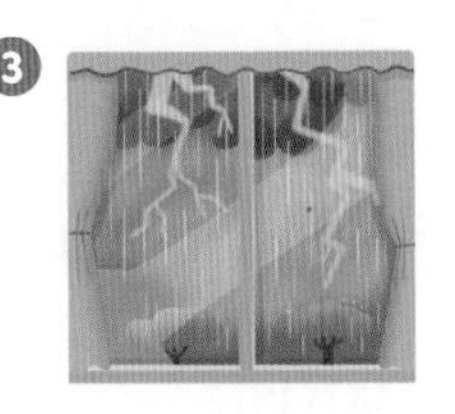
④ 
⑤ 

1. You ________________ drink this water. (may / may not)
2. We ________________ enter the room. (may / may not)
3. You ________________ open the window. (may / may not)
4. He ________________ eat healthy food. (should / should not)
5. They ________________ play mobile games in class. (should / should not)

B 우리말과 같은 뜻이 되도록 괄호 안의 표현들 중 알맞은 것을 고르세요.

1. 너는 오늘 밤 여기서 자도 된다.
   → You (must / may / should) sleep here tonight.
2. 우리는 서로에게 인사를 해야 한다.
   → We (may / can / should) say hello to each other.
3. 그들은 거리에서 큰 소리로 노래를 부르지 않는 게 좋다.
   → They (cannot / should not / don't have to) sing loudly on the street.

C 질문에 대한 대답을 완성하세요.

1. A : May I drink this juice? 이 주스 마셔도 돼요?
   B : Yes, ____________ ____________.
2. A : May I turn on the TV? TV 틀어도 될까요?
   B : No, you ____________ ____________.

healthy 건강에 좋은 in class 수업 중에 say hello to ~에게 인사하다, 안부를 전하다 each other 서로 loudly 큰 소리로 turn on ~를 켜다, 틀다

D 우리말과 같은 뜻이 되도록 보기 속 동사들과 조동사 may나 should를 써서 문장을 완성하세요.

1. 너희는 오늘 집에 일찍 가도 된다.
   → You ____________ ____________ home early today.
2. 점심 먹고 나서 아이스크림 먹어도 돼요?
   → ____________ I ____________ ice cream after lunch?
3. 식사 전에는 손을 씻는 게 좋습니다.
   → You ____________ ____________ your hands before eating.
4. 내일 우산을 갖고 가야 할까요?
   → ____________ I ____________ an umbrella tomorrow?
5. 이 도시 사람들은 이 도서관을 이용해도 됩니다.
   → People in this town ____________ ____________ this library.

보기

wash
go
use
eat
bring

E 우리말 뜻을 참고하여 밑줄 친 부분을 바르게 고치세요.

1. She may uses my phone now. 그녀는 지금 내 전화를 사용해도 된다.
   →
2. You don't may go to bed after 10. 너는 10시 넘어서 잠자리에 들면 안 된다.
   →
3. May have I this doll? 저 이 인형 가져도 돼요?
   →
4. You should being quiet in the museum. 박물관에서는 조용히 해야 한다.
   →
5. You don't should touch the paintings. 그림에 손을 대면 안 됩니다.
   →

eating 식사 town 읍, (소)도시 doll 인형 touch 만지다, 손대다 painting 그림

STEP 3 술술 쓰기가 되는 문장 연습

A 각 문장을 지시대로 다시 쓰세요.

1. You may play badminton here. 너는 여기서 배드민턴을 쳐도 된다.
   부정문 ______________________

2. I may read the book aloud. 나는 그 책을 소리 내어 읽어도 된다.
   의문문 ______________________

3. He may ride this bike. 그는 이 자전거를 타도 된다.
   의문문 ______________________

4. I should not talk about the event. 나는 그 일에 대해 이야기하면 안 된다.
   긍정문 ______________________

5. We should stay home today. 우리는 오늘 집에 있어야 한다.
   부정문 ______________________

B 주어진 단어들을 바르게 배열하여 우리말과 같은 뜻이 되도록 문장을 완성하세요.

1. 당신은 이 우산을 써도 됩니다. (may / this umbrella / you / use / .)
   → ______________________

2. 저녁 식사 후에 TV 봐도 될까요? (after dinner / watch TV / may / I / ?)
   → ______________________

3. 지금은 극장에 들어가면 안 됩니다. (you / go / may not / into the theater / now / .)
   → ______________________

4. 규칙적으로 식사를 하는 게 좋다. (regularly / you / eat / should / .)
   → ______________________

5. 수업 중에 떠들지 말아야 한다. (should not / in class / you / make noise / .)
   → ______________________

aloud 소리 내어, 큰 소리로 event 사건, 일, 행사 stay 머무르다, 계속 있다 regularly 규칙적으로 make noise 떠들다

C 그림을 보고 조동사 may와 주어진 동사들을 사용하여 손님과 점원의 대화를 완성하세요.

1\. Hello. ______ I ______ you? (help)

2\. ______ ______ ______ this on? (try)

3\. You ______ ______ this fitting room. (use)

4\. ______ ______ ______ by credit card? (pay)

D 그림을 보고 조동사 should와 주어진 동사들을 사용하여 엄마와 지미의 대화를 완성하세요.

Mom : Jimmy, eat your salad.

Jimmy : I don't want it. I want a hamburger and Coke.

Mom : You ______ ______ ______ fast food often. (eat) You ______ ______ your milk and eat the salad. (drink)

Jimmy : Okay. After lunch, may I play mobile games?

Mom : First, you ______ ______ your homework. (do) Also you ______ ______ a shower. (take) Then you may play mobile games.

try ~ on ~을 입어보다 fitting room 탈의실 pay (돈을) 지불하다 credit card 신용카드 salad 샐러드 hamburger 햄버거 fast food 패스트푸드 often 자주 first 먼저; 첫 번째의 also 또한, 게다가

실전 테스트

1-3 우리말과 같은 뜻이 되도록 빈칸에 들어갈 말로 알맞은 것을 고르세요.

1

그 도서관의 책들을 읽어도 됩니다.

You ________ read the books in the library.

① must ② may
③ have to ④ should
⑤ may not

2

너는 그와 영어로 이야기할 수 있니?

________ you talk with him in English?

① May ② Must
③ Do ④ Can
⑤ Should

3

운동을 규칙적으로 하는 게 좋다.

You ________ exercise regularly.

① can ② do
③ should ④ must
⑤ may

4 밑줄 친 부분의 의미로 맞지 않은 것을 고르세요.

① I have to go home now. (~해도 된다)

② You must not go out after 10. (~하면 안 된다)

③ She doesn't have to come today. (~하지 않아도 된다)

④ You should go to bed early. (~하는 게 좋다)

⑤ I cannot understand his words. (~할 수 없다)

5 빈칸에 들어갈 말로 바르게 짝지어진 것을 고르세요.

- She may ________ water after 12 o'clock.
- John has to ________ his room.

① drinks - cleans
② drinks - clean
③ drinking - clean
④ drink - cleaning
⑤ drink - clean

6 빈칸에 알맞은 것을 고르세요.

A: Can you play soccer after school?
B: No. I ________ go home early today.

① can ② may ③ do
④ have ⑤ have to

7-8 각 문장의 해석으로 가장 알맞은 것을 고르세요.

7

You should not drink too much Coke.

① 너는 콜라를 너무 많이 마실 수 없다.
② 너는 콜라를 너무 많이 마시지 않는 게 좋다.
③ 너는 너무 많은 콜라를 마시지 않아도 된다.
④ 너는 콜라를 너무 많이 마시지 않는다.
⑤ 너는 콜라를 너무 많이 마시지 않기로 했다.

8

You don't have to do it today.

① 너는 오늘 그걸 하면 안 된다.
② 너는 오늘 그걸 할 수 없다.
③ 너는 오늘 그걸 하지 않을 것이다.
④ 너는 오늘 그걸 하지 않아도 된다.
⑤ 너는 오늘 그걸 하지 않기로 했다.

9 밑줄 친 단어와 바꿔 쓸 수 있는 것을 고르세요.

He <u>must</u> wash his sneakers.

① may ② can ③ have to
④ has to ⑤ cannot

* sneakers 운동화

10 빈칸에 들어갈 말로 바르게 짝지어진 것을 고르세요.

• We ________ be quiet in the library.
• ________ you speak Korean?

① can - Have
② may - Have
③ should - Does
④ should - Can
⑤ do - Can

11 빈칸에 들어갈 수 <u>없는</u> 것을 고르세요.

David ________ wash his socks.

① can ② must
③ should ④ should not
⑤ have to

* socks 양말

12 다음 중 틀린 문장을 고르세요.

① Julia can play not the guitar.
② We must start now.
③ You must not open the door.
④ I don't have to buy a red pen.
⑤ May I use this computer?

13 다음 중 올바른 문장을 고르세요.

① Jimmy have to do his homework.
② You don't must be late for school.
③ You should wear sunglasses.
④ Can you making a snowman?
⑤ Thomas may stays at my house.

* wear sunglasses 선글라스를 쓰다

14-16 우리말을 영어로 바르게 옮긴 것을 고르세요.

14

그는 내일 6시에 일어나야 한다.

① He gets up at 6 tomorrow.
② He has to get up at 6 tomorrow.
③ He may get up at 6 tomorrow.
④ He must not get up at 6 tomorrow.
⑤ He doesn't have to get up at 6 tomorrow.

15

우리는 여기에서 기다리지 않아도 된다.

① We cannot wait here.
② We may not wait here.
③ We must not wait here.
④ We should not wait here.
⑤ We don't have to wait here.

16

너는 거짓말을 하면 안 된다.

① You cannot lie.
② You will not lie.
③ You don't have to lie.
④ You must not lie.
⑤ You should lie.

17 다음 문장을 바르게 고치는 방법으로 알맞은 것을 고르세요.

You have not to go to his house.

① have not to를 don't have to로 고친다.
② to go를 go로 고친다.
③ have not을 not have로 고친다.
④ have not to를 don't have로 고친다.
⑤ go를 going으로 고친다.

18 빈칸에 알맞은 말을 써 넣어 대화를 완성하세요.

A: Can your sister speak English?
B: No, ________ ________.

19-20 우리말 뜻에 맞도록 틀린 부분을 바르게 고쳐 문장을 다시 쓰세요.

19
You don't should make noise.
떠들면 안 됩니다.
→ ________________

20
May I using your eraser?
네 지우개 좀 써도 되니?
→ ________________

* eraser 지우개

21 주어진 단어들을 사용하여 우리말과 같은 뜻이 되도록 문장을 완성하세요.

그 아이는 자기 이름을 쓰지 못한다.
(write, his name)
→ The child ________________
________________.

* child 아이, 어린이

22-23 주어진 단어들을 바르게 배열하여 우리말과 같은 뜻이 되도록 문장을 완성하세요.

22
너는 매일 밤 양치질을 해야 한다.
(every night / you / brush your teeth / must / .)
→ ________________
____

23
늦게 자지 않는 게 좋다.
(should / late / you / go to bed / not / .)
→ ________________
____

24-25 우리말과 같은 뜻이 되도록 빈칸에 알맞은 말을 써 넣어 문장을 완성하세요.

24
창문을 닫지 않아도 됩니다.
→ You ________ ________
________ ________ the window.

25
제가 질문 하나 해도 될까요?
→ ________ ________ ask you a question?

Word List Chapter 2

앞에서 배운 단어를 한 번 더 확인하고 어렵거나 모르는 단어는 다시 공부하세요.

- [ ] basketball 농구
- [ ] build 짓다, 세우다
- [ ] carrot 당근
- [ ] concert 콘서트, 음악회
- [ ] enter 들어가다
- [ ] exam 시험
- [ ] feed 먹이를 주다
- [ ] jump 점프하다
- [ ] museum 박물관, 미술관
- [ ] pass 통과하다
- [ ] pet 반려동물
- [ ] promise 약속
- [ ] reply to ~에 대답하다, 답장을 보내다
- [ ] rule 규칙
- [ ] solve 풀다, 해결하다
- [ ] touch 만지다, 손대다
- [ ] umbrella 우산
- [ ] vegetable 채소
- [ ] bring 데려오다
- [ ] call 전화하다
- [ ] carry 들다, 운반하다
- [ ] cross 건너다, 횡단하다
- [ ] event 사건, 일, 행사
- [ ] exercise 운동하다
- [ ] fix 고치다, 수리하다
- [ ] lock 잠그다
- [ ] parents 부모님
- [ ] pay (돈을) 지불하다
- [ ] problem 문제
- [ ] quiet 조용한
- [ ] return 돌려주다
- [ ] save 아끼다, 모으다
- [ ] stay 머무르다, 계속 있다
- [ ] train 기차
- [ ] understand 이해하다
- [ ] word 단어

be동사의 과거형

동영상 강의

Unit 1. be동사의 과거형

Unit 2. be동사 과거형의 부정문과 의문문

be동사 am/is의 과거형은 was, are의 과거형은 were로, '~였다', '(~에) 있었다', '(상태가) ~했다'라는 뜻이에요. '나는 유치원생이었다.', '나는 교실에 있었다.', '나는 행복했다.'처럼 과거의 상태를 설명할 수 있어요.

UNIT 1 be동사의 과거형

1 be동사의 과거형

'~였다, (~에) 있었다, (상태가) ~했다'라고 과거의 상태를 말할 때 be동사의 과거형을 써요. be동사의 과거형은 was와 were 두 가지예요.
주어가 I, he, she, it, 그리고 단수 명사일 때는 was를 쓰고, 주어가 you, we, they, 그리고 복수 명사일 때는 were를 써요.

1인칭 단수	I was
2인칭 단수	you were
3인칭 단수	he/she/it was
복수	we/you/they were

I **was** 10 years old last year. 나는 작년에 열 살이었다.
You **were** at home yesterday. 너는 어제 집에 있었다.
They **were** sad at the news. 그들은 그 소식을 듣고 슬펐다.
It **was** sunny that day. 그날은 날씨가 맑았다.
There **was** a theater here then. 그때는 여기에 극장이 있었다.

⊙ 과거형에 자주 쓰는 표현들

yesterday 어제　last ~ 지난 ~에　that day 그날　at that time 그때　then 그때　in 연도 ~년에

2 be동사의 현재형과 과거형 비교

현재의 사실이나 상태를 말할 때 be동사의 현재형을 쓰고, 어제, 지난주, 몇 달 전, 작년 등 과거의 사실이나 과거의 상태를 나타낼 때 be동사의 과거형을 써요.

be동사의 현재형	am, are, is	현재의 사실, 상태
be동사의 과거형	was, were	과거의 사실, 상태

현재형 현재의 사실이나 상태를 말해요.

I **am** sleepy now. 나는 지금 졸리다.
Emily **is** American. 에밀리는 미국인이다.

과거형 과거의 사실이나 상태를 말해요.

I **was** sick yesterday. 나는 어제 아팠다.
They **were** at the park then. 그들은 그때 공원에 있었다.

STEP 1 기초 탄탄 연습

A 빈칸에 알맞은 be동사의 과거형을 쓰세요.

1. I am → I ________
2. you are → you ________
3. he is → he ________
4. we are → we ________
5. she is → she ________
6. they are → they ________
7. Nora is → Nora ________
8. My friends are → My friends ________

B 그림을 참고하여 괄호 안에서 알맞은 be동사를 고르세요.

1. The apple (was / were) in the basket.

2. John and Andy (was / were) good friends.

3. Jennifer (was / were) a tennis player.

4. The players (was / were) thirsty.

C 각 문장이 현재의 사실인지 과거의 사실인지 √ 표시 하세요.

1. I was a student at that time. ☐ 현재 ☐ 과거
2. The bird was on the roof. ☐ 현재 ☐ 과거
3. This book is very interesting. ☐ 현재 ☐ 과거
4. The students were in the classroom. ☐ 현재 ☐ 과거

basket 바구니 player 선수 thirsty 목이 마른 roof 지붕 interesting 재미있는

STEP 2 규칙 적용 연습

A 그림을 참고하여 빈칸에 알맞은 be동사의 과거형을 쓰세요.

① 2017 ②  ③ 

④  ⑤ 

1. I ____________ a kindergartner in 2017.

2. Carl ____________ very busy yesterday.

3. The girls ____________ at the bus stop then.

4. There ____________ a lot of flowers in the garden.

5. Jimin and Jun ____________ baseball players.

B 우리말과 같은 뜻이 되도록 괄호 안의 표현들 중 알맞은 것을 고르세요.

1. 나는 지금 열세 살이다.
   → I (am / was) 13 years old now.

2. 박 선생님은 작년에 우리 과학 선생님이셨다.
   → Ms. Park (is / was) our science teacher last year.

3. 그들은 어젯밤에 극장에 있었다.
   → They (are / were) at the theater last night.

4. 오늘은 한국에서 어린이날이다.
   → Today (is / was) Children's Day in Korea.

5. 10년 전에 여기 테마파크가 있었다.
   → There (is / was) a theme park here 10 years ago.

kindergartner 유치원생 busy 바쁜 bus stop 버스 정류장 a lot of 많은 garden 정원 science 과학 last year 작년 last night 어젯밤(에) theme park 테마파크 ago ~ 전에

C 우리말과 같은 뜻이 되도록 빈칸에 알맞은 주어와 be동사를 쓰세요.

1. 나는 오늘 오후에 집에 있었다.

→ ________ __________ at home this afternoon.

2. 너는 그때 나와 같은 반이었잖아.

→ ________ __________ my classmate at that time.

3. 그는 19세기의 유명한 피아니스트였다.

→ ________ __________ a famous pianist in the 19th century.

4. 우리는 그해에 정말 행복했다.

→ ________ __________ really happy that year.

5. 그들은 수업이 끝난 후에 도서관에 있었다.

→ ________ __________ at the library after school.

D 주어진 문장을 과거형으로 바꿀 때 빈칸에 알맞은 표현을 쓰세요.

1. I am 12 years old. 나는 열두 살이다.

과거형 ________________ 12 years old.

2. There is a tall tower in this city. 이 도시에는 높은 탑이 있다.

과거형 ________________ a tall tower in this city.

3. The vegetables are fresh. 그 채소들은 신선하다.

과거형 ____________________________ fresh.

4. We are at the amusement park. 우리는 놀이공원에 있다.

과거형 ________________ at the amusement park.

5. Stella and Jenny are classmates. 스텔라와 제니는 같은 반 친구다.

과거형 ________________________________ classmates.

classmate 같은 반 친구 famous 유명한 pianist 피아니스트 century 세기 really 정말로
tower 탑 city 도시 fresh 신선한 amusement park 놀이공원

STEP 3 술술 쓰기가 되는 문장 연습

A 우리말 뜻을 참고하여 틀린 부분을 바르게 고쳐 문장을 다시 쓰세요.

1. I am really tired last night. 나는 어젯밤에 정말 피곤했다.
   → ______________________________

2. It was cloudy in Seoul now. 지금 서울은 흐리다.
   → ______________________________

3. My cat is nine years old last year. 내 고양이는 작년에 아홉 살이었다.
   → ______________________________

4. He were a nurse at that time. 그는 그때 간호사였다.
   → ______________________________

5. John and Olivia was at the restaurant last night. 존과 올리비아는 어젯밤에 그 식당에 있었다.
   → ______________________________

B 주어진 단어들을 바르게 배열하여 우리말과 같은 뜻이 되도록 문장을 완성하세요.

1. 나의 할아버지는 농부셨다. (was / my / a farmer / grandfather / .)
   → ______________________________

2. 그때 우리는 중학생이었다. (middle school students / were / then / we / .)
   → ______________________________

3. 마당에는 나무가 두 그루 있었다. (two trees / were / in the yard / there / .)
   → ______________________________

4. 그 가수의 목소리는 무척 아름다웠다. (very beautiful / the singer's / was / voice / .)
   → ______________________________

5. 케이크와 빵은 맛있었다. (were / the cake / delicious / and bread / .)
   → ______________________________

tired 피곤한 restaurant 식당 farmer 농부 middle school 중학교 yard 마당 beautiful 아름다운 singer 가수 voice 목소리 delicious 맛있는 bread 빵

C 빈칸에 알맞은 be동사의 과거형을 써서 오늘의 일기를 완성하세요.

May 23rd, Saturday

Sunny

I went to the zoo today.

There ________ many animals.

There ________ giraffes, elephants, lions, tigers, giant pandas, peacocks, and so on.

The giraffe ________ tall, and its neck ________ really long.

The elephant ________ big, and its nose ________ long.

The lions and tigers ________ cool but scary.

There ________ two giant pandas, and they ________ very cute.

The peacock's wings ________ very colorful.

I had a good time at the zoo.

I want to go there again.

May 5월 animal 동물 giant panda 대왕판다 peacock 공작(새) and so on 등등
cool 멋진 scary 무서운 wing 날개 colorful 화려한 again 또, 다시

UNIT 2 be동사 과거형의 부정문과 의문문

1 be동사 과거형의 부정문

be동사 과거형의 부정문은 was와 were 뒤에 not을 써서 만들어요. **'~가 아니었다, (~에) 없었다, (상태가) ~하지 않았다'**라는 뜻이에요. was not은 wasn't로, were not은 weren't로 줄여 쓰는 경우가 많아요.

1인칭 단수	I was not
2인칭 단수	you were not
3인칭 단수	he/she/it was not
복수	we/you/they were not

I was not a middle school student in 2020.
나는 2020년에 중학생이 아니었다.

You were not in the house at that time. 너는 그때 집에 없었다.

She was not tall last year. 그녀는 작년에 키가 크지 않았다.

The book wasn't interesting. 그 책은 재미없었다.

The boys weren't in the classroom. 그 남자아이들은 교실에 없었다.

2 be동사 과거형의 의문문

'~였나요?, (~에) 있었나요?, (상태가) ~했나요?'라고 과거의 사실이나 상태에 대해 묻는 의문문은 Was 또는 Were를 주어 앞에 써서 만들어요.

질문 ~였나요?	긍정 대답 네.	부정 대답 아니요.
Was I ~?	Yes, you were.	No, you were not.
Were you ~?	Yes, I was.	No, I was not.
Was he/she/it ~?	Yes, he/she/it was.	No, he/she/it was not.
Were we/you/they ~?	Yes, you/we/they were.	No, you/we/they were not.

was not은 wasn't로, were not은 weren't로 줄여 쓸 수 있어요.

Was I wrong? → 긍정 Yes, you were. 부정 No, you weren't.
내가 틀렸었나요?

Were you sick yesterday? → 긍정 Yes, I was. 부정 No, I wasn't.
너 어제 아팠니?

Was Phillip in the kitchen? → 긍정 Yes, he was. 부정 No, he wasn't.
필립이 주방에 있었어요?

Were the students late? → 긍정 Yes, they were. 부정 No, they weren't.
그 학생들이 늦었나요?

STEP 1 기초 탄탄 연습

A 올바른 문장에 √ 표시 하세요.

1. ☐ The movie not was so sad.
   ☐ The movie was not so sad.

2. ☐ Was Olivia at home last Saturday?
   ☐ Were Olivia at home last Saturday?

3. ☐ Was the sandwiches delicious?
   ☐ Were the sandwiches delicious?

B 그림을 보고 괄호 안에서 알맞은 것을 고르세요.

① ② ③ ④ ⑤

1. It (was / wasn't) rainy.

2. She (was / wasn't) tall.

3. They (weren't / were) at the library.

4. (Was / Were) the balloon purple?

5. (Was / Were) the boys in the playground?

C 질문에 대한 대답으로 알맞은 것을 골라 √ 표시 하세요.

1. Was the book interesting? 그 책 재미있었니?
   ☐ Yes, it is. ☐ No, it wasn't.

2. Were you at the movie theater then? 너는 그때 극장에 있었니?
   ☐ Yes, you were. ☐ Yes, I was.

sad 슬픈 rainy 비가 오는 balloon 풍선 purple 보라색의; 보라색

STEP 2 규칙 적용 연습

A 그림을 보고 보기에서 알맞은 단어를 빈칸에 넣어 문장을 완성하세요. (필요한 경우 한 단어를 2번 이상 사용하세요.)

보기 was wasn't were weren't

1. They __________ at the pool. They __________ at the museum.
2. The boy __________ happy. He __________ sad.
3. __________ you sick yesterday? ----- Yes, I was.
4. __________ your grandfather a doctor? ----- Yes, he was.
5. __________ the children at the school cafeteria? ----- Yes, they were.

B 우리말 뜻에 맞도록 괄호 안에서 알맞은 것을 고르세요.

1. I (am not / was not) surprised at the news then. 나는 그때 그 소식에 놀라지 않았다.
2. The children (are not / were not) on the beach now. 그 아이들은 지금 해변에 있지 않다.
3. Annie and Eric (are not / were not) middle school students last year.
   애니와 에릭은 작년에 중학생이 아니었다.

C 질문에 대한 대답을 완성하세요.

1. A: Was Tony at the concert yesterday? 토니는 어제 그 콘서트에 있었니?
   B: Yes, he __________.
2. A: Were the shoes expensive? 그 신발은 비쌌나요?
   B: No, they __________.

sick 아픈 school cafeteria 학교 식당 surprised 놀란 be surprised at ~에 놀라다 news 소식 shoes 신발 expensive 비싼

D 우리말과 같은 뜻이 되도록 빈칸에 알맞은 단어를 쓰세요.

1. 수학 시험은 어렵지 않았다.
   → The math exam __________ __________ difficult.

2. 그들은 그 빵집에 있지 않았다.
   → They __________ __________ at the bakery.

3. 너는 그때 서울에 있었니?
   → __________ __________ in Seoul at that time?

4. 그녀가 작년에 그들의 음악 선생님이었나요?
   → __________ __________ their music teacher last year?

5. 그들은 그 학교의 학생들이었나요?
   → __________ __________ students of that school?

E 우리말 뜻을 참고하여 틀린 부분을 찾아 바르게 고치세요.

1. He not was kind. 그는 친절하지 않았다.
   __________ → __________

2. The bread weren't sweet. 그 빵은 달지 않았다.
   __________ → __________

3. You were tired last night? 너는 어젯밤에 피곤했니?
   __________ → __________

4. Were the moon round? 달이 둥글었나요?
   __________ → __________

5. Do the apples big? 그 사과들은 컸어요?
   __________ → __________

difficult 어려운 bakery 빵집 kind 친절한 sweet 달콤한 moon 달 round 둥근

STEP 3 술술 쓰기가 되는 문장 연습

A 각 문장을 지시대로 다시 쓰세요.

1. He was a famous scientist. 그는 유명한 과학자였다.
   부정문 ______________________________

2. The movie was very funny. 그 영화는 무척 웃겼다.
   부정문 ______________________________

3. You were in New York then. 너는 그때 뉴욕에 있었다.
   의문문 ______________________________

4. The concert was really good. 그 음악회는 정말 좋았다.
   의문문 ______________________________

5. They were at the bookstore at that time. 그들은 그때 그 서점에 있었다.
   의문문 ______________________________

B 주어진 단어들을 바르게 배열하여 우리말과 같은 뜻이 되도록 문장을 완성하세요.

1. 그 남자아이는 졸리지 않았다. (not / the boy / sleepy / was / .)
   → ______________________________

2. 그의 어머니는 부산 출신이 아니셨다. (from Busan / not / his mother / was / .)
   → ______________________________

3. 우리는 어젯밤에 그의 집에 있지 않았다. (not / last night / we / at his house / were / .)
   → ______________________________

4. 너 그때 정말 행복했니? (were / then / really happy / you / ?)
   → ______________________________

5. 미나는 작년에 너랑 같은 반이었니? (Mina / was / last year / your classmate / ?)
   → ______________________________

scientist 과학자 funny 우스운, 재미있는 bookstore 서점 sleepy 졸린 be from ~ 출신이다, ~에서 오다

C 빈칸에 알맞은 대명사와 be동사의 긍정형이나 부정형을 써서 유나와 친구의 대화를 완성하세요.

Hi, Yuna! How was your vacation?

It ______ great. I visited my aunt in Europe.

______ you in England?

No, ______ ______. I was in France.
My aunt lives in France.

Oh, does she? How was France?
______ it beautiful?

Yes, ______ ______. France in autumn was very beautiful.

D 부부가 경찰에게 사라진 반지에 대해 이야기하고 있어요. 빈칸에 알맞은 대명사와 be동사의 긍정형이나 부정형을 써서 부부와 경찰의 대화를 완성하세요.

Until yesterday, my wife's ring was in the box, but it ______ there this morning.

______ you at home last night?

No, I ______. My wife and I were at a party. We ______ at home last night.

Ma'am, where were you this morning? ______ ______ home?

Yes, I ______ in our bedroom.

vacation 방학 visit 방문하다, 찾아가다 aunt 이모, 고모, 숙모, 아주머니 Europe 유럽
England 잉글랜드, 영국 France 프랑스 autumn 가을 until (때) ~까지 ring 반지 bedroom 침실

실전 테스트

1-2 빈칸에 들어갈 말로 알맞은 것을 고르세요.

1

It ________ sunny yesterday.

① is ② are
③ am ④ was
⑤ were

2

________ the children in the playground then?

① Am ② Are
③ Is ④ Was
⑤ Were

3-4 주어진 문장을 과거형으로 바르게 바꾼 것을 고르세요.

3

I am not a pilot.

① I did not a pilot.
② I don't be a pilot.
③ I am do not a pilot.
④ I didn't be a pilot.
⑤ I was not a pilot.

* pilot (비행기) 조종사

4

Are the girls at the library?

① Was the girls at the library?
② Were the girls at the library?
③ The girls was at the library?
④ Did the girls at the library?
⑤ Are the girls were at the library?

5 빈칸에 들어갈 말로 바르게 짝지어진 것을 고르세요.

• I ________ seven years old last year.
• They ________ in Seoul now.

① am - were ② is - are
③ was - are ④ am - are
⑤ was - were

6 빈칸에 공통으로 들어갈 말을 고르세요.

• Tom and Jerry ________ good friends then.
• Anne, ________ you at home last Sunday?

① were ② is
③ are ④ was
⑤ do

* Sunday 일요일

7 빈칸에 들어갈 말이 나머지와 다른 하나를 고르세요.

① She ________ sick last night.
② ________ your mother at home at that time?
③ I ________ not a student in 2015.
④ James and I ________ in America that year.
⑤ It ________ cold yesterday.

8-10 주어진 문장을 지시대로 바르게 바꾼 것을 고르세요.

8

It was hot yesterday. 의문문

① Is it hot yesterday?
② Wasn't hot yesterday?
③ Was hot it yesterday?
④ Was it hot yesterday?
⑤ Did it was hot yesterday?

9

The sky was blue. 부정문

① The sky not was blue.
② The sky did not blue.
③ The sky was not blue.
④ The sky did not was blue.
⑤ The sky was did not blue.

10

Your sister was a dentist. 의문문

① Is your sister a dentist?
② Your sister a dentist was?
③ Was your sister a dentist?
④ Does your sister be a dentist?
⑤ Do your sister a dentist?

* dentist 치과의사

11-12 빈칸에 들어갈 수 없는 것을 고르세요.

11

There was ________.

① a table
② a subway station
③ some books
④ some milk
⑤ Joseph

12

They were in Paris ________.

① last year ② last month
③ last week ④ yesterday
⑤ now

13 다음 중 밑줄 친 부분이 틀린 문장을 고르세요.

① Ms. Wilson was from Canada.
② They were at the school cafeteria.
③ Was it cold last night?
④ Were you surprised at the news?
⑤ The dog and the cat was on the sofa together.

* be surprised at ~에 놀라다

14-15 다음 중 틀린 문장을 고르세요.

14 ① I was an elementary school student last year.
② Was that your book?
③ There was five people in the room.
④ They were not home then.
⑤ The girls were late for school.

15 ① I was in Jeonju in 2020.
② They were busy yesterday.
③ Were you with them then?
④ Mr. Anderson was not a teacher last year.
⑤ The children not were in the classroom.

16-17 질문에 대한 대답으로 알맞은 것을 고르세요.

16

A: Was the movie interesting?
B: ______

① Yes, it is.
② Yes, it was.
③ No, it isn't.
④ No, it was.
⑤ No, it weren't.

17

A: Were you late for the concert yesterday?
B: ______

① Yes, you were.
② No, I wasn't.
③ Yes, I am.
④ No, you weren't.
⑤ No, you were.

18 대답을 보고 질문으로 알맞은 것을 고르세요.

A: ______
B: Yes, she was.

① Is she a nurse?
② Was the man kind?
③ Was your sister a cook?
④ Were the girls happy?
⑤ Was it sunny yesterday?

19 우리말 뜻에 맞도록 틀린 부분을 바르게 고쳐 문장을 다시 쓰세요.

Tim and Grace was in Korea last year.
팀과 그레이스는 작년에 한국에 있었다.

→ ______________________

____

20-21 우리말을 영어로 옮길 때 빈칸에 알맞은 단어를 쓰세요.

20 그녀는 어제 아프지 않았다.

→ She ________ ________ sick yesterday.

21 그들은 오늘 오전에 학교에 있었나요?

→ ________ ________ at school this morning?

22-23 주어진 단어들을 바르게 배열하여 우리말과 같은 뜻이 되도록 문장을 완성하세요.

22 어제 더웠나요?

(hot / it / yesterday / was / ?)

→ ______________________

____

23 그들은 그때 화가 나지 않았다.

(at that time / angry / not / they / were / .)

→ ______________________

____

24-25 주어진 단어들을 사용하여 우리말과 같은 뜻의 영어 문장을 쓰세요.

24 그 축구 선수는 키가 컸나요?

(the soccer player)

→ ______________________

25 그 꽃들은 흰색이 아니었다.

(the flowers, white)

→ ______________________

Word List Chapter 3

앞에서 배운 단어를 한 번 더 확인하고 어렵거나 모르는 단어는 다시 공부하세요.

- [ ] animal 동물
- [ ] balloon 풍선
- [ ] beautiful 아름다운
- [ ] busy 바쁜
- [ ] city 도시
- [ ] colorful 화려한
- [ ] difficult 어려운
- [ ] famous 유명한
- [ ] funny 우스운, 재미있는
- [ ] interesting 재미있는
- [ ] roof 지붕
- [ ] sad 슬픈
- [ ] science 과학
- [ ] singer 가수
- [ ] sweet 달콤한
- [ ] tired 피곤한
- [ ] vacation 방학
- [ ] voice 목소리
- [ ] autumn 가을
- [ ] basket 바구니
- [ ] bread 빵
- [ ] century 세기
- [ ] classmate 같은 반 친구
- [ ] delicious 맛있는
- [ ] expensive 비싼
- [ ] fresh 신선한
- [ ] garden 정원
- [ ] restaurant 식당
- [ ] round 둥근
- [ ] scary 무서운
- [ ] sick 아픈
- [ ] surprised 놀란
- [ ] thirsty 목이 마른
- [ ] tower 탑
- [ ] visit 방문하다, 찾아가다
- [ ] wing 날개

CHAPTER 4

일반동사의 과거형

동영상 강의

일반동사의 과거형은 과거에 '~했다'라는 뜻으로,

'말했다, 먹었다, 뛰었다'처럼 과거에 했던 행동이나 '사랑했다, 원했다'처럼 과거의 상태를 나타낼 때 써요.

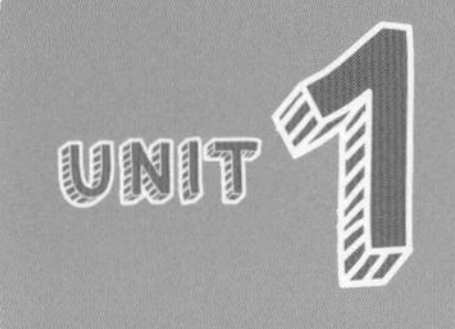

일반동사의 과거형 (규칙 변화)

1 일반동사의 과거형 (규칙 변화)

과거에 했던 행동이나 과거의 상태는 일반동사의 과거형으로 나타내요. 과거에 '~했다'라는 뜻이에요.
대부분 동사의 과거형은 동사원형에 -ed나 -d를 붙여서 만들어요.

대부분의 동사 → 동사원형 + -ed	help (돕다) → helped look (보다) → looked play (놀다) → played walk (걷다) → walked watch (보다) → watched	listen (듣다) → listened open (열다) → opened talk (말하다) → talked want (원하다) → wanted work (일하다) → worked
-e로 끝나는 동사 → 동사원형 + -d	close (닫다) → closed like (좋아하다) → liked love (사랑하다) → loved	dance (춤추다) → danced live (살다) → lived move (움직이다) → moved
<자음+-y>로 끝나는 동사 → y를 i로 바꾸고 -ed	cry (울다) → cried study (공부하다) → studied worry (걱정하다) → worried	dry (말리다, 건조시키다) → dried try (시도하다, 노력하다) → tried
<모음1+자음1>로 끝나는 동사 → 자음을 한 번 더 쓰고 -ed	drop (떨어뜨리다) → dropped stop (멈추다) → stopped	plan (계획하다) → planned

I watched the movie last night. 나는 어젯밤에 그 영화를 보았다.
She liked cartoons in her childhood days. 그녀는 어린 시절에 만화를 좋아했다.
We studied math together yesterday. 우리는 어제 수학을 함께 공부했다.
The woman dropped the flower vase. 그 여성은 꽃병을 떨어뜨렸다.

2 현재형과 과거형 비교

현재형	• 현재 반복적으로 하는 행동 • 현재의 상태, 사실	I go jogging every morning. (현재 반복적으로 하는 행동) 나는 매일 아침 조깅을 간다. She likes K-pop. (현재의 사실, 상태) 그녀는 케이팝을 좋아한다.
과거형	• 과거에 했던 행동 • 과거의 상태, 사실	I played soccer yesterday. (과거에 했던 행동) 나는 어제 축구를 했다. He hated vegetables as a child. (과거의 사실, 상태) 그는 어렸을 때 채소를 싫어했다.

STEP 1 기초 탄탄 연습

A 주어진 동사들의 과거형을 쓰세요.

1. 
open
____

2.  stop
____

3. 
cry
____

4. 
dance
____

5. 
listen
____

6. 
study
____

7. 
talk
____

8. 
play
____

B 각 문장을 읽고 과거형 동사에 동그라미 한 후 그 뜻을 쓰세요.

1. He worked for a bank. (뜻 :)
2. I closed the door of the room. (뜻 :)
3. She watched TV in the living room. (뜻 :)
4. The woman loved her child so much. (뜻 :)

C 우리말과 같은 뜻이 되도록 괄호 안에서 알맞은 동사를 고르세요.

1. 그녀는 한 노부인을 도와드렸다. She (helps / helped) an old lady.
2. 그는 다른 사람들을 자주 돕는다. He often (helps / helped) other people.
3. 나는 부산에 산다. I (live / lived) in Busan.
4. 그는 제주도에 살았다. He (lives / lived) on Jeju Island.

bank 은행 living room 거실 lady 여성, 여자분 other 다른 island 섬

STEP 2 규칙 적용 연습

A 주어진 동사들의 과거형을 알맞은 자리에 넣어 문장을 완성하세요.

live   rain   drop   dry   clean

1. Tommy ______________ his room.
2. It ______________ a lot yesterday.
3. She ______________ the wet T-shirt.
4. The boy ______________ the glass.
5. They ______________ in Finland.

B 우리말과 같은 뜻이 되도록 보기에서 알맞은 동사를 골라 과거형 문장을 완성하세요.

1. I ______________ for the train station at 9.
   나는 9시에 기차역으로 출발했다.
2. I ______________ at the train station at 10.
   나는 10시에 기차역에 도착했다.
3. My dad ______________ tomato pasta.
   우리 아빠는 토마토 파스타를 요리하셨다.
4. We ______________ it very much.
   우리는 그것을 무척 맛있게 먹었다.
5. The children ______________ with sand.
   그 아이들은 모래를 가지고 놀았다.
6. Then they ______________ their hands.
   그다음에 그들은 손을 씻었다.

보기
arrive
cook
enjoy
play
start
wash

a lot 많이 wet 젖은 glass 유리잔 start for ~로 출발하다 arrive 도착하다 train station 기차역 pasta 파스타 enjoy 즐기다, 맛있게 먹다 sand 모래

C 각 문장이 현재를 나타내는지 과거를 나타내는지 골라 √ 표시 하세요.

1. The boys played soccer after school. ☐ 현재 ☐ 과거
2. Many people hope for world peace. ☐ 현재 ☐ 과거
3. They moved to Shanghai in 2019. ☐ 현재 ☐ 과거
4. She works at a broadcasting station. ☐ 현재 ☐ 과거
5. I usually played the piano in the morning. ☐ 현재 ☐ 과거

D 우리말과 같은 뜻이 되도록 보기에서 알맞은 동사를 골라 과거형 문장을 완성하세요.

보기 study talk close look plan paint

1. 그 남자아이는 창밖을 내다보았다.
   → The boy ________ out the window.
2. 그 여자아이는 교실 문을 닫았다.
   → The girl ________ the classroom door.
3. 우리는 가족 소풍을 계획했다.
   → We ________ a family picnic.
4. 그들은 그 음악회에 대해 이야기했다.
   → They ________ about the concert.
5. 그는 어젯밤에 수학 시험 공부를 했다.
   → He ________ for a math test last night.
6. 우리 아빠는 어제 벽에 페인트 칠을 하셨다.
   → My dad ________ the walls yesterday.

hope for ~을 바라다 world peace 세계 평화 move to ~로 이주하다 broadcasting station 방송국 usually 보통 plan 계획하다 paint 페인트를 칠하다, (물감으로) 그리다 picnic 소풍 wall 벽

STEP 3 술술 쓰기가 되는 문장 연습

A 우리말 뜻에 맞도록 틀린 부분을 바르게 고쳐 문장을 다시 쓰세요.

1. I live in Daegu three years ago. 나는 3년 전에 대구에 살았다.
→ ______________________

2. She baked bread every day. 그녀는 매일 빵을 굽는다.
→ ______________________

3. He often plays badminton last year. 그는 작년에 자주 배드민턴을 쳤다.
→ ______________________

4. The car stops in front of their house. 그 차는 그들의 집 앞에서 멈췄다.
→ ______________________

5. Julia talks with Annie for two hours. 줄리아는 애니와 2시간 동안 이야기했다.
→ ______________________

B 주어진 단어들을 바르게 배열하여 우리말과 같은 뜻이 되도록 문장을 완성하세요.

1. 나는 밤에 음악을 들었다. (listened / at night / I / to music / .)
→ ______________________

2. 지난 겨울에는 눈이 많이 왔다. (snowed / last winter / it / a lot / .)
→ ______________________

3. 그 아기는 한 시간 동안 울었다. (cried / for an hour / the baby / .)
→ ______________________

4. 그는 다음 시험에 대해 걱정했다. (the next exam / worried about / he / .)
→ ______________________

5. 그들은 가게 문을 오전 10시에 열었다. (at 10 a.m. / they / the store / opened)
→ ______________________

in front of ~ 앞에(서) for + 시간 ~ 동안 hour 시간 next 다음의 worry 걱정하다 about ~에 대해 store 가게, 상점

C 주어진 동사를 알맞은 형태로 빈칸에 넣어 소년과 기타의 이야기를 완성하세요.

Guitar and Me

I ____________(start) playing the guitar at the age of 10. I ____________(learn) to play the guitar from my dad. My dad often ____________(play) the guitar at home. I ____________(listen) to his guitar and ____________(enjoy) it very much. So I ____________(ask) him to teach me to play it.

D 보기의 동사들을 알맞은 형태로 빈칸에 넣어 레오나르도 다빈치의 이야기를 완성하세요.

보기 paint study live die design

Leonardo da Vinci

Leonardo da Vinci was a painter, sculptor, scientist, and inventor. He was born in Italy in 1452 and ____________ in Italy all his life. He ____________ art under a famous artist in his teens. He ____________ the *Mona Lisa* and *The Last Supper*. He also ____________ a flying machine and a helicopter. He ____________ in 1519 at 67.

age 나이 at the age of ~살의 나이에, ~살 때에 design 설계하다, 디자인하다 painter 화가 sculptor 조각가 inventor 발명가 be born 태어나다 all one's life 평생 artist 예술가, 화가 teens 십대 시절 machine 기계 helicopter 헬리콥터

UNIT 2 일반동사의 과거형 (불규칙 변화)

1 일반동사의 과거형 (불규칙 변화)

모든 동사가 -ed나 -d가 붙어서 과거형이 되는 것은 아니에요. 다른 형태로 변화해서 과거형이 되는 동사들도 있어요.

1) 현재형과 과거형이 완전히 다른 동사

begin (시작하다, 시작되다) → began	buy (사다) → bought	come (오다) → came
do (하다) → did	draw (그리다) → drew	drink (마시다) → drank
drive (운전하다) → drove	eat (먹다) → ate	feel (느끼다) → felt
find (찾다) → found	get (얻다) → got	give (주다) → gave
go (가다) → went	have (가지고 있다) → had	hear (듣다) → heard
know (알다) → knew	lose (잃어버리다) → lost	make (만들다) → made
meet (만나다) → met	run (달리다) → ran	see (보다) → saw
sell (팔다) → sold	sing (노래하다) → sang	sit (앉다) → sat
sleep (자다) → slept	speak (말하다) → spoke	take (잡다, 얻다) → took
teach (가르치다) → taught	tell (말하다) → told	write (쓰다) → wrote

2) 현재형과 과거형이 같은 동사

cut (자르다) → cut	hit (치다) → hit	hurt (다치게 하다) → hurt
put (놓다, 두다) → put	read (읽다) → read	set (놓다) → set

read는 현재형과 과거형의 발음이 달라요.
현재형 [riːd], 과거형 [red]

I **did** my homework before dinner. 나는 저녁 식사 전에 숙제를 했다.
She **went** to the gym this morning. 그녀는 오늘 아침에 체육관에 갔다.
The boy **ate** an egg sandwich for lunch. 그 남자아이는 점심으로 달걀 샌드위치를 먹었다.
I **saw** a Christmas tree in front of the coffee shop. 나는 그 커피숍 앞에서 크리스마스트리를 보았다.
We **read** books at the library today. 우리는 오늘 도서관에서 책을 읽었다.

STEP 1 기초 탄탄 연습

A 각 동사의 과거형을 쓰세요.

1. have ____________ 2. get ____________

3. find ____________ 4. put ____________

5. tell ____________ 6. speak ____________

7. know ____________ 8. sit ____________

B 그림을 참고하여 괄호 안에서 알맞은 동사를 고르세요.

1. I (read / readed) a book this morning.

2. She (goes / went) shopping an hour ago.

3. Ben (eats / ate) pizza for lunch yesterday.

4. My mom (makes / made) a doll for me last month.

C 각 문장을 읽고 과거형 동사에 동그라미 하고 그 뜻을 쓰세요.

1. She drank a glass of milk. (뜻 :)

2. We met in front of the library. (뜻 :)

3. They slept in a tent that night. (뜻 :)

4. Mr. Kim taught science last year. (뜻 :)

go shopping 쇼핑하러 가다 tent 텐트

STEP 2 규칙 적용 연습

A 그림을 참고하여 괄호 안에서 알맞은 동사를 고르세요.

1.

ⓐ She (goed / went) to bed at 10 last night.

ⓑ She (getted / got) up at 6 this morning.

2.

ⓐ I (sang / singed) my favorite song.

ⓑ I (feeled / felt) really good.

3.

ⓐ His friends (comed / came) to his birthday party.

ⓑ They (ate / eated) cake and had a good time.

B 주어진 동사의 과거형을 빈칸에 써서 문장을 완성하세요.

1. I ______________ a movie last Sunday. (see)
   나는 지난 일요일에 영화를 한 편 보았다.

2. He ______________ on the sofa last night. (sleep)
   그는 어젯밤에 소파에서 잤다.

3. My brother ______________ his wallet today. (find)
   우리 오빠는 오늘 그의 지갑을 찾았다.

4. Emily ______________ cereal for breakfast this morning. (eat)
   에밀리는 오늘 아침에 아침 식사로 시리얼을 먹었다.

5. The boy ______________ his homework after dinner last night. (do)
   그 남자아이는 어젯밤에 저녁을 먹고 나서 숙제를 했다.

6. She ______________ history at a middle school for 20 years. (teach)
   그녀는 한 중학교에서 20년 동안 역사를 가르쳤다.

favorite 특히[매우] 좋아하는 birthday 생일 wallet 지갑 cereal 시리얼 history 역사

C 우리말과 같은 뜻이 되도록 보기에서 알맞은 동사를 골라 과거형 문장을 완성하세요.

보기 hear read write give

1. 우리는 그 소문을 들었다.
   → We ________________ the rumor.

2. 나는 어젯밤에 그에게 편지를 썼다.
   → I ________________ a letter to him last night.

3. 그는 그 어린 여자아이에게 곰 인형을 주었다.
   → He ________________ a teddy bear to the little girl.

4. 그 여자아이는 《이상한 나라의 앨리스》라는 책을 읽었다.
   → The girl ________________ a book called *Alice in Wonderland*.

D 두 문장 중 그림을 바르게 묘사한 문장을 골라 √ 표시 하세요.

1.
☐ She ran with her dog.
☐ She walked with her dog.

2.
☐ He painted a picture.
☐ He saw a picture.

3.
☐ I bought an ice cream.
☐ I sold an ice cream.

4.

☐ She learned English.
☐ She taught English.

rumor 소문 teddy bear 곰 인형 called ~라는 (이름의)

STEP 3 술술 쓰기가 되는 문장 연습

A 우리말 뜻에 맞도록 틀린 부분을 바르게 고쳐 문장을 다시 쓰세요.

1. I cutted the tomatoes in half. 나는 토마토를 반으로 잘랐다.
→

2. Andrew maked a snowman yesterday. 앤드류는 어제 눈사람을 만들었다.
→

3. Betty went jogging every morning. 베티는 매일 아침 조깅하러 간다.
→

TIP 습관이나 반복적인 행동은 현재형을 써서 나타내요.

4. I sitted at the back of the classroom. 나는 교실 뒤쪽에 앉았다.
→

5. He readed a lot of books in his school days. 그는 학창 시절에 책을 많이 읽었다.
→

B 주어진 단어들을 바르게 배열하여 우리말과 같은 뜻이 되도록 문장을 완성하세요.

1. 그 아이들은 크리스마스 캐럴을 불렀다. (the children / a Christmas carol / sang / .)
→

2. 제니퍼가 나에게 웃긴 이야기를 하나 해주었다. (a funny story / Jennifer / told me / .)
→

3. 나는 펜과 공책을 많이 가지고 있었다. (a lot of / had / I / pens and notebooks / .)
→

4. 그는 오늘 저녁 7시에 집에 왔다. (came home / he / at 7 this evening / .)
→

5. 그녀는 저녁으로 햄버거와 감자튀김을 샀다.
(for dinner / she / hamburgers and fries / bought / .)
→

in half 반으로 go jogging 조깅하러 가다 back 뒤 in one's school days 학창 시절에 story 이야기 fries 감자튀김

C 두 친구가 주말을 어떻게 보냈는지에 대해 대화를 나누고 있어요. 보기의 동사들을 알맞은 형태로 바꾸어 대화를 완성하세요.

보기 drink set go have eat

Hi, Carol. How was your weekend?

Great! I ________ camping with my mom, dad, and dog, Toto. We ________ up a tent together. I ________ meat and ramyeon. I also ________ hot chocolate.

Wow. You really ________ a good time!

D 보기의 동사들을 알맞은 형태로 바꾸어 지난 크리스마스 이야기를 완성하세요.

Last Christmas

Last Christmas was a white Christmas. It ________ snowing on Christmas Eve. On Christmas morning, I ________ Christmas cards and ________ them to my parents and brother. There was a gift from Santa Claus under the Christmas tree, but I ________ it was from my parents. In the afternoon, I ________ a snowman with my brother. At night, I ________ a book about Christmas listening to Christmas carols.

보기
- begin
- give
- know
- make
- read
- write

go camping 캠핑하러 가다 set up a tent 텐트를 치다 meat 고기 ramyeon 라면
gift 선물 Santa Claus 산타클로스

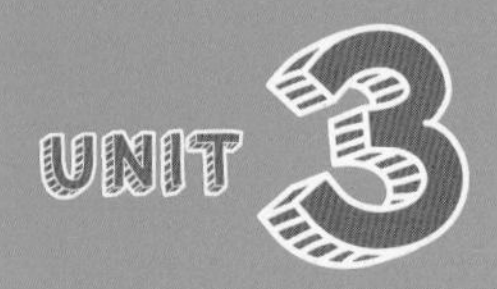

UNIT 3 일반동사 과거형의 부정문, 의문문

❶ 일반동사 과거형의 부정문 : ~하지 않았다

과거에 '**~하지 않았다**'라고 말할 때는 did not을 동사원형 앞에 써요. 주어에 상관없이 〈**did not+동사원형**〉으로 쓰고, did not은 didn't로 줄여 쓸 수 있어요.

긍정문	주어 + 동사의 과거형	~했다
부정문	주어 + did not (didn't) + 동사원형	~하지 않았다

긍정		 부정
I **took** a shower this morning. 나는 오늘 아침에 샤워를 했다.	→	I **didn't take** a shower this morning. 나는 오늘 아침에 샤워를 하지 않았다.
The girl **watched** TV last night. 그 여자아이는 어젯밤에 TV를 보았다.	→	The girl **didn't watch** TV last night. 그 여자아이는 어젯밤에 TV를 보지 않았다.
They **went** to school yesterday. 그들은 어제 학교에 갔다.	→	They **didn't go** to school yesterday. 그들은 어제 학교에 가지 않았다.

❷ 일반동사 과거형의 의문문 : ~했나요?

과거에 '**~했나요?**'라고 묻는 의문문은 did를 문장 맨 앞에 써서 〈**Did+주어+동사원형 ~?**〉으로 써요.
대답은 긍정이면 Yes, 부정이면 No로 해요.

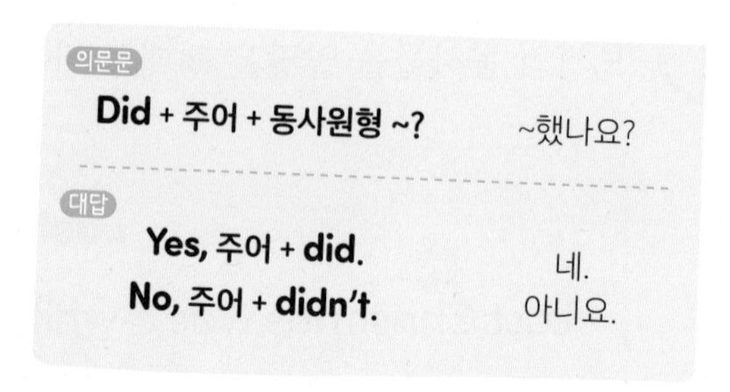

의문문	Did + 주어 + 동사원형 ~?	~했나요?
대답	Yes, 주어 + did. No, 주어 + didn't.	네. 아니요.

Did you **have** breakfast this morning? 너 오늘 아침에 아침 먹었니?
→ **Yes**, I **did**. 네, 먹었어요.
No, I **didn't**. 아니요, 먹지 않았어요.

Did she **read** the novel last week? 그녀는 지난주에 그 소설을 읽었나요?
→ **Yes**, she **did**. 네, 읽었어요.
No, she **didn't**. 아니요, 읽지 않았어요.

Did they **go** to the amusement park last weekend? 그들은 지난 주말에 놀이공원에 갔나요?
→ **Yes**, they **did**. 네, 갔어요.
No, they **didn't**. 아니요, 가지 않았어요.

STEP 1 기초 탄탄 연습

A 각 문장의 부정문이나 의문문을 완성하세요.

1. I bought a new bag. → I ________ buy a new bag.
   나는 새 가방을 사지 않았다.

2. Ben slept well last night. → ________ Ben sleep well last night?
   벤은 어젯밤에 잘 잤나요?

3. Annie drank milk today. → Annie didn't ________ milk today.
   애니는 오늘 우유를 마시지 않았다.

4. John traveled to South America. → Did John ________ to South America?
   존은 남아메리카로 여행을 갔나요?

B 각 문장을 부정문이나 의문문으로 알맞게 바꾼 문장에 √ 표시 하세요.

1. They lived in LA at that time.
   그들은 그때 LA에 살았다.
   - ☐ They not lived in LA at that time.
   - ☐ They didn't live in LA at that time.

2. It rained yesterday.
   어제 비가 왔다.
   - ☐ Did it rain yesterday?
   - ☐ Was it rained yesterday?

3. We went fishing last Saturday.
   우리는 지난 토요일에 낚시를 하러 갔다.
   - ☐ We didn't went fishing last Saturday.
   - ☐ We didn't go fishing last Saturday.

C 그림을 보고 질문에 대한 대답으로 알맞은 것에 √ 표시 하세요.

1. Did you go hiking yesterday?
   - ☐ Yes, I did.
   - ☐ No, I didn't.

2. Did Sarah finish her meal?
   - ☐ Yes, she did.
   - ☐ No, she didn't.

travel 여행하다 South America 남아메리카 go fishing 낚시하러 가다 finish 끝마치다 meal 식사

STEP 2 규칙 적용 연습

A 그림을 보고 괄호 안에서 알맞은 것을 고르세요.

❶ 
❷ 

❸ 
❹ 

❺ 

1. Olivia (ate / didn't eat) a hamburger.
2. David (had / didn't have) 10 dollars.
3. I (took / didn't take) the bus this morning.
4. Ms. Park (talked / didn't talk) in English.
5. He (cooked / didn't cook) noodles in the kitchen.

B 우리말과 같은 뜻이 되도록 보기에서 알맞은 동사를 골라 과거형 의문문을 완성하세요.

보기 drive know go wash do

1. 그녀는 손을 씻었나요?
   → ________ she __________ her hands?

2. 너 숙제했니?
   → ________ you __________ your homework?

3. 그가 네 전화번호를 알았니?
   → ________ he __________ your phone number?

4. 그들은 지난 토요일에 소풍을 갔나요?
   → ________ they __________ on a picnic last Saturday?

5. 그 남자가 스쿨버스를 운전했나요?
   → ________ the man __________ the school bus?

 dollar 달러 noodle 국수 kitchen 주방, 부엌 phone number 전화번호 go on a picnic 소풍을 가다 school bus 스쿨버스

C 빈칸을 채워서 각 문장을 부정문이나 의문문으로 바꿔 쓰세요.

1. I felt good that day. 나는 그날 기분이 좋았다.
   부정문 ____________ good that day.

2. My father worked for a post office. 나의 아버지는 우체국에서 일하셨다.
   부정문 ____________ for a post office.

3. I got up at 6 this morning. 나는 오늘 아침 여섯 시에 일어났다.
   부정문 ____________ at 6 this morning.

4. Kelly went to her aunt's house. 켈리는 자기 이모 집에 갔다.
   의문문 ____________ to her aunt's house?

5. The science class began at 2 p.m. 과학 수업은 오후 2시에 시작했다.
   의문문 ____________ at 2 p.m.?

D 그림을 보고 빈칸에 알맞은 단어를 써서 질문에 대한 대답을 완성하세요.

①
②
③
④
⑤

1. Did she go to New York last fall? ----- Yes, she ______.

2. Did you paint a picture there? ----- ______, I ______.

3. Did Mr. Kim sell fish? ----- No, ______ ______.

4. Did they run a marathon? ----- ______, they ______.

5. Did you get a good score? ----- ______, ______ ______.

post office 우체국 fall 가을 marathon 마라톤 score 점수 get a good score 좋은 점수를 받다

STEP 3 술술 쓰기가 되는 문장 연습

A 우리말 뜻을 참고하여 틀린 부분을 바르게 고쳐 문장을 다시 쓰세요.

1. I didn't studied history yesterday. 나는 어제 역사를 공부하지 않았다.
   →

2. We lived not in Seoul in 2010. 우리는 2010년에 서울에 살지 않았다.
   →

3. Did you took a shower last night? 너 어젯밤에 샤워했어?
   →

4. He did his homework after dinner? 그는 저녁 식사 후에 숙제를 했나요?
   →

5. Did you played the piano last night? 너 어젯밤에 피아노 쳤니?
   →

B 주어진 단어들을 바르게 배열하여 우리말과 같은 뜻이 되도록 문장을 완성하세요.

1. 나는 그들의 새 CD를 사지 않았다. (buy / I / their new CD / didn't / .)
   →

2. 그는 주말에는 아침을 먹지 않았다. (breakfast / eat / he / on weekends / didn't / .)
   →

3. 너는 어제 조지를 만났니? (you / did / George / meet / yesterday / ?)
   →

4. 그녀는 그 극장에서 그 영화를 보았나요?
   (watch / she / did / at the theater / the movie / ?)
   →

5. 존이 작년에 샌프란시스코로 이사 갔나요?
   (last year / did / move / John / to San Francisco / ?)
   →

C 계획표를 보고 애니가 한 일과 하지 않은 일에 대한 글을 완성하세요.

Annie's To-Do List

O	finish my science homework
O	write a blog post
X	clean my room
O	walk my dog
X	water the flowers

Annie had many things to do today. She ________ her science homework. She ________ a blog post. And she ________ her dog. But she ________ ________ her room and ________ ________ the flowers.

D 주어진 동사와 do를 알맞은 형태로 빈칸에 넣어 지난 여름방학에 대한 대화를 완성하세요. 필요한 대명사도 넣으세요.

A: Subin, did you ________ to Paris last summer? (travel)

B: Yes, I did.

A: ______ you ______ to the Louvre Museum? (go)

B: Yes, I ______.

A: ______ ______ ______ the *Mona Lisa*? (see)

B: Sure, I did.

A: Did you go up the Eiffel Tower?

B: No, I ________. I just looked at it.

list 목록　many things to do 해야 할 많은 일들　blog post 블로그 게시물[게시글]　walk 산책을 시키다　water 물을 주다　summer 여름　Louvre Museum 루브르 박물관　Eiffel Tower 에펠탑　go up ~에 올라가다　look at ~을 보다

실전 테스트

1-2 다음 중 동사의 과거형이 잘못 연결된 것을 고르세요.

1 ① put - put ② do - did
③ find - found ④ give - gived
⑤ close - closed

2 ① like - liked ② go - went
③ tell - telled ④ stop - stopped
⑤ study - studied

3 다음 중 동사의 현재형과 과거형의 형태가 다른 것을 고르세요.

① cut ② hit ③ put
④ get ⑤ set

4-5 빈칸에 들어갈 말이 바르게 짝지어진 것을 고르세요.

4
- We ________ camping last weekend.
- She ________ swimming every day.

① go - goes ② go - went
③ went - going ④ went - go
⑤ went - goes

5
- I ________ a stomachache last night.
- He didn't ________ a bike last year.

① have - has ② had - have
③ had - had ④ had - has
⑤ have - had

* have a stomachache 배가 아프다

6-7 주어진 문장을 과거형으로 바르게 바꾼 것을 고르세요.

6
I go to bed at 10.

① I did go to bed at 10.
② I was go to bed at 10.
③ I goed to bed at 10.
④ I was going to bed at 10.
⑤ I went to bed at 10.

7
She writes a lot of poems.

① She write a lot of poems.
② She wrote a lot of poems.
③ She writed a lot of poems.
④ She did writes a lot of poems.
⑤ She was write a lot of poems.

* poem 시

8 빈칸에 공통으로 들어갈 말을 고르세요.

- Chris, ________ you hear the news?
- I ________ not take a nap yesterday.

① were ② am
③ do ④ did
⑤ can

* take a nap 낮잠을 자다

9-10 주어진 문장을 지시대로 바르게 바꾼 것을 고르세요.

9

I met Jamie last Saturday. 의문문

① Do you meet Jamie last Saturday?
② Did you meet Jamie last Saturday?
③ Did you met Jamie last Saturday?
④ Were you met Jamie last Saturday?
⑤ Were you meet Jamie last Saturday?

10

The girl ran fast. 부정문

① The girl didn't ran fast.
② The girl ran not fast.
③ The girl didn't run fast.
④ The girl not ran fast.
⑤ The girl was not run fast.

11-13 빈칸에 들어갈 수 없는 것을 고르세요.

11

She ________ last year.

① lived here ② came here
③ went there ④ studied here
⑤ works here

12

We saw the movie ________.

① yesterday ② last weekend
③ in 2020 ④ tomorrow
⑤ last night

13

Did you ________ it?

① read ② see ③ made
④ buy ⑤ eat

14 다음 중 틀린 문장을 고르세요.

① We lived in Daegu last year.
② I didn't read the book.
③ Did you see the man?
④ David didn't know the woman.
⑤ She goes to the market yesterday.

* market 시장

15 밑줄 친 부분을 바르게 고친 것으로 짝지어진 것을 고르세요.

- He move here in 2020.
- The girl drawed this picture last year.

① moves - draw
② moved - drew
③ moved - draw
④ move - drew
⑤ moved - draws

16 다음 중 올바른 문장을 고르세요.

① He reads the book last week.
② We worryed about him then.
③ Did you closed the door?
④ I didn't know the answer.
⑤ She get up late this morning.

17-18 질문에 대한 대답으로 알맞은 것을 고르세요.

17

A: Did you go to college?
B: ______________________

① Yes, you did.
② Yes, I did.
③ Yes, you went.
④ No, you didn't.
⑤ No, I wasn't.

* college 대학(교)

18

A: Did Eddy make this pasta?
B: ______________________

① Yes, Eddy didn't.
② Yes, he did made.
③ Yes, he made.
④ No, he didn't.
⑤ No, he wasn't.

19-20 우리말 뜻에 맞도록 틀린 부분을 바르게 고쳐 문장을 다시 쓰세요.

19

The festival begins last Friday.
그 축제는 지난 금요일에 시작되었다.

→ ______________________

____

20

We didn't ate breakfast this morning.

우리는 오늘 아침에 아침밥을 먹지 않았다.

→ ______________________

____

21-23 우리말을 영어로 옮길 때 빈칸에 알맞은 단어를 쓰세요.

21

나는 어제 거리에서 그를 보았다.

→ I ________ him on the street ________.

22

그는 중국어를 배우지 않았다.

→ He ________ ________ Chinese.

23

너는 오늘 도서관에 갔니?

→ ________ you ________ to the library today?

24-25 주어진 단어들을 바르게 배열하여 우리말과 같은 뜻이 되도록 문장을 완성하세요.

24

너는 오늘 학교에서 점심을 먹었니?

(you / at school today / did / have lunch / ?)

→ ______________________

____

25

그녀는 지난 주말에 박물관에 가지 않았다.

(to the museum / didn't / she / last weekend / go / .)

→ ______________________

____

Word List Chapter 4

앞에서 배운 단어를 한 번 더 확인하고 어렵거나 모르는 단어는 다시 공부하세요.

- [ ] age 나이
- [ ] artist 예술가, 화가
- [ ] birthday 생일
- [ ] dance 춤추다
- [ ] drop 떨어뜨리다
- [ ] favorite 특히 좋아하는
- [ ] gift 선물
- [ ] hour 시간
- [ ] kitchen 주방, 부엌
- [ ] machine 기계
- [ ] other 다른
- [ ] picnic 소풍
- [ ] rumor 소문
- [ ] score 점수
- [ ] store 가게, 상점
- [ ] try 시도하다, 노력하다
- [ ] wallet 지갑
- [ ] wet 젖은
- [ ] arrive 도착하다
- [ ] bank 은행
- [ ] close 닫다
- [ ] design 설계하다, 디자인하다
- [ ] dry 말리다
- [ ] finish 끝마치다
- [ ] history 역사
- [ ] island 섬
- [ ] lady 여성, 여자분
- [ ] meat 고기
- [ ] peace 평화
- [ ] plan 계획하다
- [ ] sand 모래
- [ ] start 출발하다
- [ ] travel 여행하다
- [ ] wall 벽
- [ ] want 원하다
- [ ] worry 걱정하다

CHAPTER 5

부사

동영상 강의

Unit 1. 부사의 형태와 쓰임

Unit 2. 빈도부사

부사는 언제, 어디서, 어떻게, 얼마나 등을 나타내는 말이에요. 동사나 형용사, 다른 부사를 꾸며서 동작이나 상태에 의미를 더해줘요. '빨리 달린다', '무척 친절하다', '늦게 왔다'에서 '빨리', '무척', '늦게'가 부사예요.

UNIT 1 부사의 형태와 쓰임

① 부사

부사는 때(언제), 장소(어디서), 방법(어떻게), 정도(얼마나) 등을 나타내는 말이에요. '~**하게**'라고 해석되는 경우가 많아요.

때	now (지금) today (오늘) yesterday (어제) tomorrow (내일) soon (곧)
장소	here (여기) there (거기)
방법, 정도	very (매우) well (잘) fast (빨리) early (일찍) really (정말로) happily (행복하게) kindly (친절하게) easily (쉽게) slowly (천천히)

② 부사의 역할

부사는 문장 속에서 동사나 형용사, 다른 부사를 꾸며주는 역할을 해요. 그래서 부사가 들어가면 문장의 의미가 풍성해져요.

동사를 꾸밈
He came home late. 그는 집에 늦게 왔다.
They study English hard. 그들은 영어를 열심히 공부한다.

형용사를 꾸밈
She is very kind. 그녀는 매우 친절하다.
The movie is really funny. 그 영화는 정말 웃기다.

다른 부사를 꾸밈
He runs very fast. 그는 매우 빨리 달린다.
She sings really well. 그녀는 노래를 정말 잘 부른다.

③ 부사의 형태

부사는 형용사의 형태가 바뀌어서 만들어져요. 대부분 '형용사+-ly'로 이루어지지만, 형용사와 부사의 형태가 같은 경우도 있어요.

대부분의 부사 → 형용사+-ly	nice → nicely (멋지게, 잘) sad → sadly (슬프게) slow → slowly (천천히, 느리게)	quick → quickly (빨리, 신속하게) careful → carefully (조심스럽게, 주의 깊게) quiet → quietly (조용히)
-y로 끝나는 형용사 → y를 빼고 -ily	easy → easily (쉽게) lucky → luckily (운 좋게, 다행히)	happy → happily (행복하게)
-le로 끝나는 형용사 → e를 빼고 -y	gentle → gently (부드럽게, 온화하게)	simple → simply (단순하게)
형용사와 형태가 같은 부사	early (이른) → early (일찍) high (높은) → high (높이, 높게) hard (힘든, 어려운) → hard (열심히)	late (늦은) → late (늦게) low (낮은) → low (낮게) fast (빠른) → fast (빠르게)
형용사와 형태가 완전히 다른 부사	good (좋은) → well (잘)	

STEP 1 기초 탄탄 연습

A 각 문장에서 부사에 동그라미 하세요.

1. The baby is very cute. 그 아기는 매우 귀엽다.

2. Joe opened the door slowly. 조는 천천히 문을 열었다.

3. We met Mr. Kim yesterday. 우리는 어제 김 선생님을 만났다.

4. The girl speaks English well. 그 여자아이는 영어를 잘한다.

TIP 부사는 '언제, 어디서, 어떻게, 얼마나' 등을 나타내는 말이에요.

B 그림을 참고하여 괄호 안에서 알맞은 것을 고르세요.

1. 

The boy plays the violin (good / well).

2. 

The singer sings (beautiful / beautifully).

3. 

He gets up (early / earlily) in the morning.

4. 

The girl studies (hard / hardly) for the test.

C 각 형용사를 부사로 바꿔 쓰세요.

1. kind → ________
2. simple → ________
3. early → ________
4. lucky → ________
5. gentle → ________
6. easy → ________
7. careful → ________
8. happy → ________
9. quick → ________
10. quiet → ________

STEP 2 규칙 적용 연습

A 형용사의 부사형으로 맞는 것을 고르고 부사의 뜻을 쓰세요.

1. sad - (sad / sadly) 뜻 : ____________
2. happy - (happyly / happily) 뜻 : ____________
3. fast - (fast / fastly) 뜻 : ____________
4. good - (goodly / well) 뜻 : ____________
5. easy - (easy / easily) 뜻 : ____________
6. nice - (nice / nicely) 뜻 : ____________
7. lucky - (luckly / luckily) 뜻 : ____________
8. late - (late / latily) 뜻 : ____________
9. high - (higly / high) 뜻 : ____________
10. hard - (hard / hardy) 뜻 : ____________

B 그림을 보고 괄호 안에서 알맞은 것을 골라 빈칸에 쓰세요.

① 
② 
③ 
④ 
⑤ 

1. Turtles move ____________. (fast / slowly)
2. The baby smiled ____________. (happily / sadly)
3. She arrived at the bus stop ____________. (early / late)
4. The bird flies ____________ in the sky. (high / low)
5. The man spoke ____________. (kindly / angrily)

turtle 거북이 smile 웃다, 미소 짓다

C 밑줄 친 부사가 꾸미는 말에 동그라미 하세요.

1. Jimin studies English hard. 지민이는 영어를 열심히 공부한다.

2. She goes to school early. 그녀는 학교에 일찍 간다.

3. The book was really interesting. 그 책은 정말 재미있었다.

4. The athlete ran very fast. 그 선수는 매우 빨리 달렸다.

5. The woman spoke kindly. 그 여성은 친절하게 말했다.

TIP 부사는 동사, 형용사, 다른 부사를 꾸며줘요.

D 우리말과 같은 뜻이 되도록 알맞은 부사를 골라 빈칸에 쓰세요.

보기 quickly easily hard quietly carefully really

1. 그녀는 정말로 동물을 좋아한다.
→ She ________ likes animals.

2. 나는 그 문제를 쉽게 풀었다.
→ I solved the problem ________.

3. 그들은 지하철에서 조용히 이야기했다.
→ They talked ________ on the subway.

4. 그들은 신속하게 병원으로 갔다.
→ They went to the hospital ________.

5. 학생들은 선생님의 말씀을 주의 깊게 들었다.
→ The students listened ________ to the teacher.

6. 우리는 시험을 위해 열심히 공부했다.
→ We studied ________ for the test.

athlete 운동선수, 육상선수 hospital 병원

STEP 3 술술 쓰기가 되는 문장 연습

A 우리말 뜻을 참고하여 틀린 부분을 바르게 고쳐 문장을 다시 쓰세요.

1. The puppy is small really. 그 강아지는 정말 작다.
→ ______________________________

2. She always drives safe. 그녀는 항상 안전하게 운전한다.
→ ______________________________

3. My dad works hardly. 우리 아빠는 열심히 일하신다.
→ ______________________________

4. He opened the door easy. 그는 그 문을 쉽게 열었다.
→ ______________________________

5. Don't come home lately today. 오늘 집에 늦게 오지 마.
→ ______________________________

B 주어진 단어들을 바르게 배열하여 우리말과 같은 뜻이 되도록 문장을 완성하세요.

1. 내 동생은 춤을 잘 춘다. (dances / well / my brother / .)
→ ______________________________

2. 고래는 정말 크다. (really / whales / big / are / .)
→ ______________________________

3. 그 농구 선수는 높이 뛴다. (high / the basketball player / jumps / .)
→ ______________________________

4. 케빈은 점심을 빨리 먹는다. (quickly / Kevin / lunch / eats / .)
→ ______________________________

5. 그곳은 아주 좋은 도서관이다. (library / it / a very / good / is / .)
→ ______________________________

puppy 강아지 always 항상 safe 안전한 whale 고래 basketball player 농구 선수

C 그림 속 동물들을 보고 주어진 동사와 보기의 부사들을 사용하여 이야기를 완성하세요.

보기 fast high(2번 사용) quietly slowly

Look at the animals.

The monkey is ________ ________. (jump)

The cheetah is ________ ________. (run)

The lion is ________ ________. (sit)

The turtle is ________ ________. (move)

The eagle is ________ ________ in the sky. (fly)

D 보기의 부사들을 한 번씩 사용하여 친구를 소개하는 글을 완성하세요.

보기 early fast hard very well

My friend Min is a ________ good student.

He gets up ________ in the morning and he is never late for school.

He is diligent and studies ________.

He is good at math and speaks English ________.

He is also good at sports and he runs ________.

He is a good friend of mine.

eagle 독수리 never 절대 ~ 않는 diligent 성실한, 근면한 be good at ~를 잘하다 sports 스포츠
a friend of mine 내 친구

빈도부사

1 빈도부사

빈도부사는 어떤 행동을 얼마나 자주 하는지, 어떤 일이 얼마나 자주 일어나는지를 나타내는 부사예요.

always	항상, 언제나 (100%)
usually	보통, 대개 (90%)
often	자주 (70%)
sometimes	때때로, 가끔 (50%)
never	절대 ~ 않는 (0%)

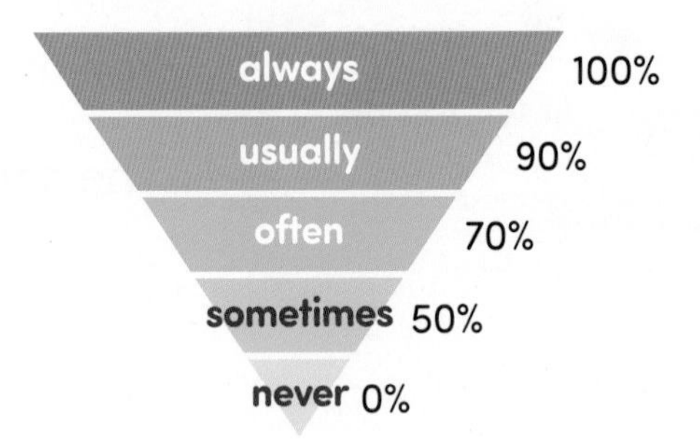

2 빈도부사의 위치

빈도부사는 어떤 동사와 함께 쓰이느냐에 따라 위치가 달라져요.
be동사와 조동사의 뒤에, 그리고 일반동사의 앞에 와요.

1) be동사와 조동사 뒤에

Mr. Wilson is always kind to his students. 윌슨 선생님은 항상 학생들에게 친절하시다.
They are usually busy on weekdays. 그들은 평일에는 보통 바쁘다.
My grandmother is often sick. 나의 할머니는 자주 편찮으시다.
You may sometimes visit my house. 너는 가끔 우리 집에 와도 돼.
Lisa is never late for school. 리사는 절대 학교에 늦지 않는다.

2) 일반동사 앞에

My mom always drinks coffee in the morning. 우리 엄마는 항상 아침에 커피를 드신다.
My dad usually has dinner at home. 우리 아빠는 보통 집에서 저녁을 드신다.
It often rains in summer in this city. 이 도시에는 여름에 비가 자주 내린다.
Mark sometimes goes to school by bicycle. 마크는 가끔 자전거로 학교에 간다.
She never eats hamburgers for lunch. 그녀는 점심으로 절대 햄버거를 먹지 않는다.

STEP 1 기초 탄탄 연습

A 밑줄 친 빈도부사의 의미로 알맞은 것을 골라 √ 표시 하세요.

1. He usually gets up early. ☐ 보통 ☐ 자주
2. Harry is always noisy. ☐ 절대 ~ 않는 ☐ 항상
3. They sometimes have lunch outside. ☐ 가끔 ☐ 자주
4. I never sing in front of people. ☐ 보통 ☐ 절대 ~ 않는
5. We often climb mountains. ☐ 항상 ☐ 자주

B 그림을 보고 괄호 안에서 알맞은 빈도부사를 골라 빈칸에 쓰세요.

❶ | √ | √ | √ | √ | √ | √ | √ |
❷ | √ | | √ | √ | | √ | √ |
❸ | | √ | | | √ | | √ |
❹ | | | | | | | |

1. He ______________ wears a yellow T-shirt. (always / often)
2. I ______________ looked at the moon at night. (often / never)
3. I ______________ cook at home. (sometimes / usually)
4. She ______________ goes to school alone. (usually / never)

C 각 문장에서 주어진 빈도부사가 들어갈 자리를 골라 동그라미 하세요.

1. Mr. Williams ❶ is ❷ busy ❸ on Mondays. 윌리엄 씨는 월요일에 (항상) 바쁘다. (always)
2. She ❶ is ❷ tired ❸ in the evening. 그녀는 저녁에 (보통) 피곤하다. (usually)
3. They ❶ go ❷ hiking ❸ on weekends. 그들은 주말에 (자주) 등산을 간다. (often)
4. You ❶ may ❷ eat out ❸ alone. 너는 (가끔) 혼자 외식해도 된다. (sometimes)
5. My mom ❶ takes ❷ a ❸ nap. 우리 엄마는 낮잠을 (절대 안) 주무신다. (never)

noisy 시끄러운 outside 밖에(서) climb 오르다 mountain 산 eat out 외식하다 alone 혼자

STEP 2 규칙 적용 연습

A 그림을 보고 알맞은 빈도부사를 빈칸에 넣어 문장을 완성하세요.

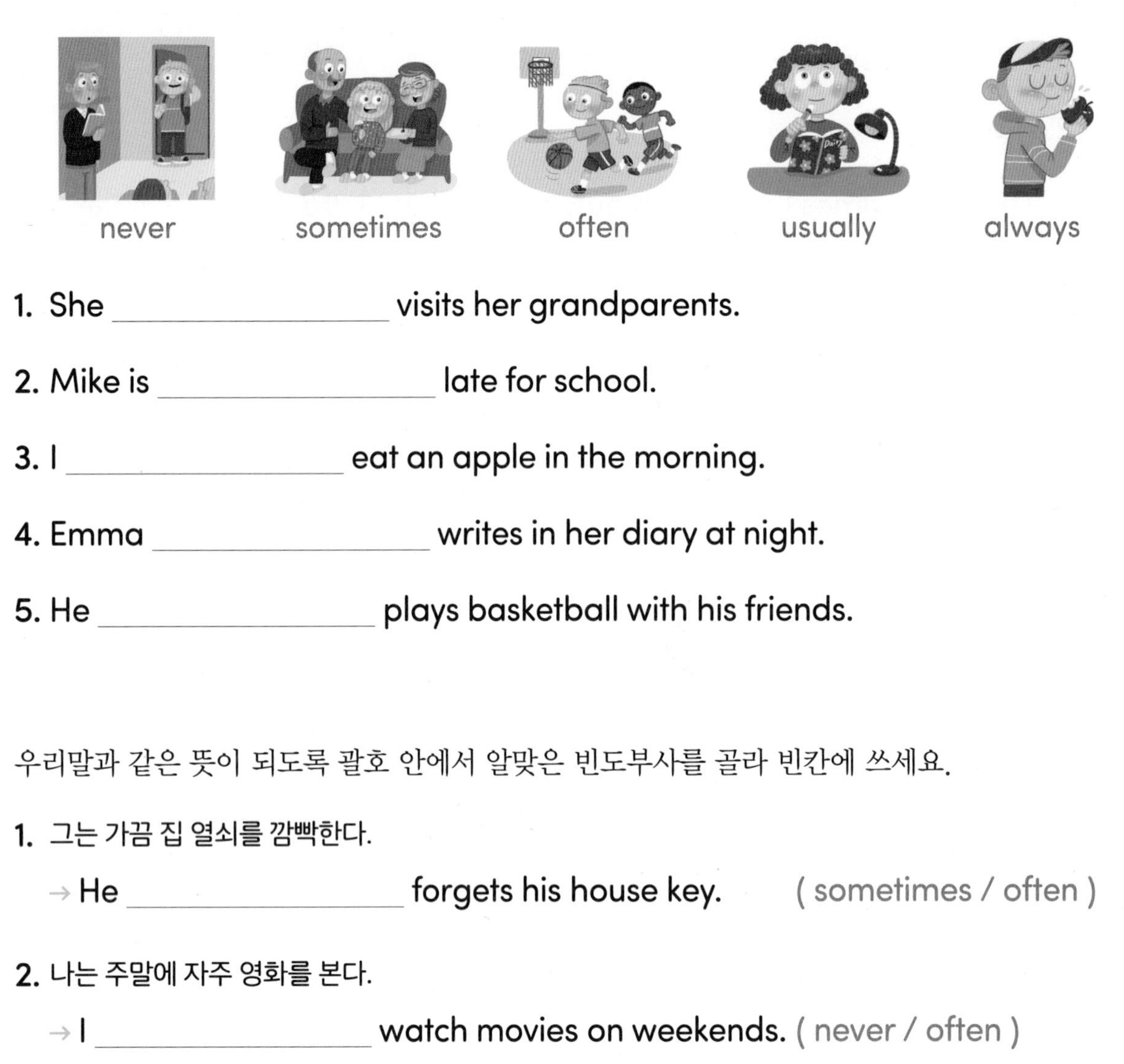

1. She ________________ visits her grandparents.
2. Mike is ________________ late for school.
3. I ________________ eat an apple in the morning.
4. Emma ________________ writes in her diary at night.
5. He ________________ plays basketball with his friends.

B 우리말과 같은 뜻이 되도록 괄호 안에서 알맞은 빈도부사를 골라 빈칸에 쓰세요.

1. 그는 가끔 집 열쇠를 깜빡한다.
   → He ________________ forgets his house key. (sometimes / often)
2. 나는 주말에 자주 영화를 본다.
   → I ________________ watch movies on weekends. (never / often)
3. 우리 오빠는 절대 우유를 마시지 않는다.
   → My brother ________________ drinks milk. (always / never)
4. 그들은 보통 일요일에는 집에 있다.
   → They ________________ stay home on Sundays. (usually / often)

grandparents 조부모 write in one's diary 일기를 쓰다 forget 잊어버리다 key 열쇠

C 각 문장에서 주어진 빈도부사가 들어갈 자리에 √ 표시 하세요.

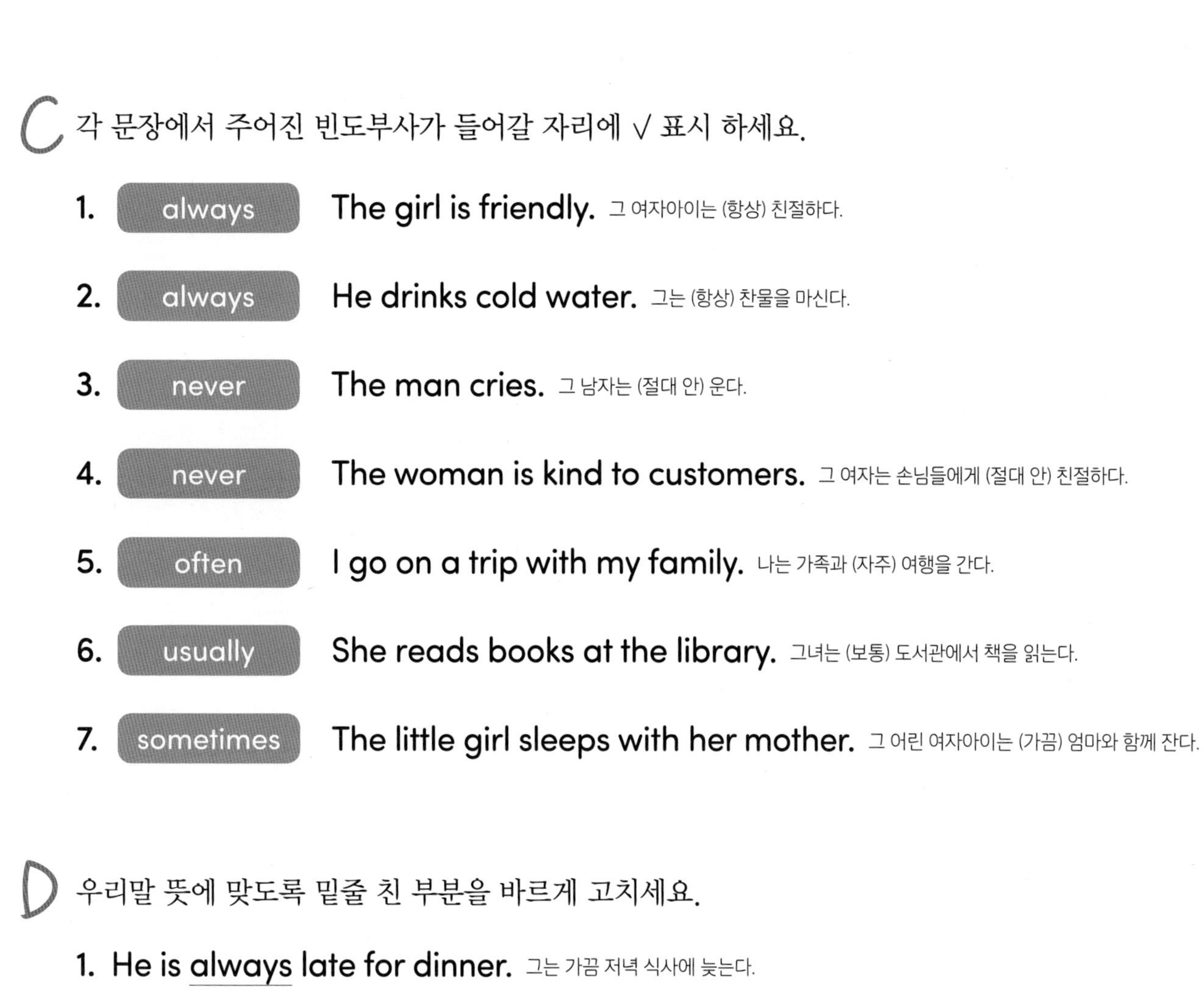

1. always — The girl is friendly. 그 여자아이는 (항상) 친절하다.
2. always — He drinks cold water. 그는 (항상) 찬물을 마신다.
3. never — The man cries. 그 남자는 (절대 안) 운다.
4. never — The woman is kind to customers. 그 여자는 손님들에게 (절대 안) 친절하다.
5. often — I go on a trip with my family. 나는 가족과 (자주) 여행을 간다.
6. usually — She reads books at the library. 그녀는 (보통) 도서관에서 책을 읽는다.
7. sometimes — The little girl sleeps with her mother. 그 어린 여자아이는 (가끔) 엄마와 함께 잔다.

D 우리말 뜻에 맞도록 밑줄 친 부분을 바르게 고치세요.

1. He is always late for dinner. 그는 가끔 저녁 식사에 늦는다.

→

2. I never eat lunch at the cafeteria. 나는 보통 구내식당에서 점심을 먹는다.

→

3. You can often come to our house. 너는 항상 우리 집에 와도 돼.

→

4. She sometimes takes a shower after dinner. 그녀는 자주 저녁 식사 후에 샤워를 한다.

→

5. I usually play mobile games at school. 나는 절대 학교에서 모바일 게임을 하지 않는다.

→

friendly 친절한, 상냥한 customer 손님, 고객 trip 여행 go on a trip 여행을 가다
cafeteria 구내식당, 셀프서비스 식당

STEP 3 술술 쓰기가 되는 문장 연습

A 우리말 뜻을 참고하여 틀린 부분을 바르게 고쳐 문장을 다시 쓰세요.

1. The man reads never books. 그 남자는 전혀 책을 읽지 않는다.
→ ______________________________

2. She sometimes is late for appointments. 그녀는 가끔 약속에 늦는다.
→ ______________________________

3. I run always in the park in the morning. 나는 아침에 항상 공원에서 달린다.
→ ______________________________

4. We usually are at home after 7 p.m. 우리는 보통 저녁 7시 이후에는 집에 있다.
→ ______________________________

5. Often Robin watches movies on Netflix. 로빈은 넷플릭스에서 자주 영화를 본다.
→ ______________________________

B 주어진 단어들을 바르게 배열하여 우리말과 같은 뜻이 되도록 문장을 완성하세요.

1. 우리는 가끔 자전거를 탄다. (bicycles / sometimes / we / ride / .)
→ ______________________________

2. 그 아이는 절대 가지를 먹지 않는다. (the child / eats / never / eggplants / .)
→ ______________________________

3. 나는 아침에 항상 조깅하러 간다. (in the morning / always / I / go jogging / .)
→ ______________________________

4. 그들은 보통 버스로 학교에 간다. (they / go to school / usually / by bus / .)
→ ______________________________

5. 애니는 집에서 자주 그림을 그린다. (Annie / at home / draws pictures / often / .)
→ ______________________________

 appointment (만날) 약속 eggplant 가지

C 에밀리의 주간 실천표를 보고 보기의 빈도부사를 한 번씩 사용하여 글을 완성하세요.

	MON	TUE	WED	THU	FRI	SAT	SUN
get up at 7	O	O	O	O	O	O	
eat breakfast	O	O	O	O	O	O	O
go swimming	O		O		O		
read books		O	O		O	O	O
go to bed after 10 p.m.							

Emily __________ __________ up at 7 in the morning.

She __________ __________ breakfast.

She __________ __________ swimming.

She __________ __________ books.

She __________ __________ to bed after 10 p.m.

보기
always
usually
often
sometimes
never

D 취미 생활의 빈도를 나타낸 표를 보고 보기의 빈도부사를 한 번씩 사용하여 글을 완성하세요.

보기 always never often sometimes

✔✔✔	cook
✔✔✔ ✔	watch a movie
✔✔✔ ✔✔✔	play with my cat
	play soccer

I have many hobbies. I like to play with my cat. I __________ play with my cat after school. I like movies, so I __________ watch them. I also like cooking and I __________ cook with my mom. But I don't like sports and I ____ ______ play soccer.

hobby 취미 cooking 요리

실전 테스트

1 다음 중 부사가 아닌 것을 고르세요.

① often ② really ③ quickly
④ early ⑤ easy

2 다음 중 형용사와 부사가 잘못 짝지어진 것을 고르세요.

① simple - simply
② kind - kindly
③ fast - fast
④ early - earlily
⑤ happy - happily

3 다음 문장에서 부사를 고르세요.

The picture on the wall is very beautiful.

① the ② on ③ is
④ very ⑤ beautiful

4 다음 중 형용사와 부사 두 가지로 모두 쓰이는 것이 아닌 것을 고르세요.

① early ② fast ③ late
④ hard ⑤ good

5 밑줄 친 부분이 부사인 것을 모두 고르세요.

① We arrived there at 11 p.m.
② She is always friendly to students.
③ There is a delicious sandwich.
④ I don't feel good today.
⑤ I never go hiking alone.

6 빈칸에 알맞은 것을 고르세요.

The man speaks English ________ well.

① with ② good ③ bad
④ really ⑤ here

7 빈칸에 들어갈 수 없는 것을 고르세요.

I can make toast ________.

① now ② well ③ here
④ quickly ⑤ always

8-9 우리말을 영어로 바르게 옮긴 것을 고르세요.

8

그는 나의 질문에 친절하게 대답했다.

① He answered my question kind.
② He answered my kind question.
③ He answered my question kindly.
④ He kind answered my question.
⑤ He answered my kindly question.

9

소피아는 항상 일찍 잠자리에 든다.

① Sophia always goes to bed early.
② Always Sophia goes to bed early.
③ Sophia goes always to bed early.
④ Sophia always go early to bed.
⑤ Sophia always goes to early bed.

10 주어진 빈도부사가 들어갈 자리를 고르세요.

Jennifer ① watches ② YouTube ③ videos ④ after dinner ⑤.
(sometimes)

11-12 빈칸에 들어갈 말이 바르게 짝지어진 것을 고르세요.

11

• My English teacher speaks ________.
• The man works ________.

① fast - hardly
② fastly - hard
③ fastly - hardly
④ hard - fast
⑤ fast - hard

12

• She is ________ late for the meeting.
• He passed the test ________.

① some - easy
② sometimes - easy
③ sometime - easily
④ sometimes - easily
⑤ some - easily

13 두 문장이 반대의 의미가 되도록 빈칸에 알맞은 말을 고르세요.

> He walks slowly.
> ↔ He walks ________.

① early ② fastly ③ fast
④ late ⑤ hard

14 밑줄 친 부사의 역할이 주어진 문장의 부사와 다른 것을 고르세요.

> They listened to the man carefully.

① The girl smiled happily.
② She quickly answered the phone.
③ The boy can jump high.
④ The movie was really sad.
⑤ My mom swims well.

15 밑줄 친 부분이 올바른 문장을 고르세요.

① She rides a bike fastly.
② This sandwich tastes well.
③ I can solve the problem easy.
④ The girl plays the piano beautifully.
⑤ He helped the old woman kind.

16 다음 중 틀린 문장을 고르세요.

① They speak quietly.
② She always is busy.
③ He usually eats quickly.
④ We never drink coffee.
⑤ I often get up late.

17 다음 4가지 일을 가장 자주 하는 일부터 순서대로 나열하세요.

> ① I often take a walk with my dog.
> ② I always have breakfast.
> ③ I sometimes go camping.
> ④ I never go to bed before 10 p.m.

(→ → →)

18 다음 문장을 바르게 고치는 방법으로 알맞은 것을 고르세요.

> She goes sometimes fishing with her father.

① goes를 went로 고친다.
② goes sometimes를 sometimes goes로 고친다.
③ fishing을 to fish로 고친다.
④ fishing을 to fishing으로 고친다.
⑤ with를 of로 고친다.

19 두 문장이 같은 뜻이 되도록 빈칸에 알맞은 동사와 부사를 쓰세요.

Mike is a fast runner.
= Mike ________ ________.

20-21 우리말을 영어로 옮길 때 빈칸에 알맞은 단어를 쓰세요.

20 비행기가 하늘 높이 난다.
→ The plane flies ________ in the sky.

21 그녀는 자주 늦게 잠자리에 든다.
→ She ________ goes to bed ________.

22-23 우리말 뜻에 맞도록 틀린 부분을 바르게 고쳐 문장을 다시 쓰세요.

22 They talked quiet in the library.
그들은 도서관에서 조용히 이야기했다.
→ ________________

23 She usually is busy on weekdays.
그녀는 평일에 보통 바쁘다.
→ ________________

* weekday 평일

24-25 주어진 단어들을 바르게 배열하여 우리말과 같은 뜻이 되도록 문장을 완성하세요.

24 그 남자아이는 춤을 매우 잘 춘다.
(well / the boy / dances / very / .)
→ ________________

25 나는 점심 식사 후에 항상 산책을 한다.
(after lunch / I / take a walk / always / .)
→ ________________

Word List Chapter 5

앞에서 배운 단어를 한 번 더 확인하고 어렵거나 모르는 단어는 다시 공부하세요.

☐	alone	혼자	☐	always	항상, 언제나
☐	appointment	약속	☐	athlete	운동선수, 육상선수
☐	carefully	조심스럽게	☐	climb	오르다
☐	customer	손님, 고객	☐	diligent	성실한, 근면한
☐	eagle	독수리	☐	easily	쉽게
☐	forget	잊어버리다	☐	friendly	친절한, 상냥한
☐	gently	부드럽게, 온화하게	☐	happily	행복하게
☐	hard	열심히	☐	hobby	취미
☐	hospital	병원	☐	key	열쇠
☐	low	낮은, 낮게	☐	mountain	산
☐	never	절대 ~ 않는	☐	noisy	시끄러운
☐	often	자주	☐	outside	밖에(서)
☐	puppy	강아지	☐	quickly	빨리, 신속하게
☐	safe	안전한	☐	simply	단순하게
☐	slowly	천천히	☐	smile	웃다, 미소 짓다
☐	sometimes	가끔	☐	soon	곧
☐	trip	여행	☐	usually	보통, 대개
☐	weekday	평일	☐	whale	고래

CHAPTER 6

전치사

Unit 1. 시간의 전치사

Unit 2. 위치, 장소의 전치사

전치사는 명사 앞에 쓰여서 시간, 장소, 방법 등을 나타내는 말이에요.
우선 시간, 날짜, 요일, 계절, 연도 등을 나타내는 전치사와 위치나 장소를 나타내는 전치사에 대해 배워요.

시간의 전치사

1 전치사

전치사는 **명사 앞**에 쓰여서 **시간, 장소, 방법** 등을 나타내는 말이에요. 시간을 나타내는 말 앞에는 다음과 같이 at, on, in, before, after, for 등의 전치사가 쓰여요.

2 시간의 전치사 at, on, in

at	시간 앞에	at 5 o'clock (5시에)	at 11:30 (11시 30분에)	
	특정한 시점 앞에	at noon (정오에(낮 12시에)) at night (밤에)	at midnight (자정에(밤 12시에)) at dawn (새벽에)	
on	날짜, 요일 앞에	on May 1st (5월 1일에)	on Sunday (일요일에)	
	특정한 날 앞에	on one's birthday (~의 생일에) on Christmas Day (크리스마스 날에)	on Children's Day (어린이날에)	
in	월, 계절, 연도 앞에	in December (12월에)	in spring (봄에)	in 2023 (2023년에)
	아침, 오후, 저녁 앞에	in the morning (아침에) in the evening (저녁에)	in the afternoon (오후에)	

I usually get up at 6 o'clock. 나는 보통 6시에 일어난다.
He doesn't drink milk at night. 그는 밤에는 우유를 마시지 않는다.
She was born on February 7th. 그녀는 2월 7일에 태어났다.
He takes drum lessons on Saturdays. 그는 토요일에 드럼 강습을 받는다.
Thanksgiving Day is in November. 추수감사절은 11월에 있다.

'~월에'라고 말할 때는 in을 쓰지만 '~월 ~일에'라고 말할 때는 on을 쓴다는 점을 기억하세요.

3 시간의 전치사 before, after, for

before	~ 전에	before 10 o'clock (10시 전에)	before sunrise (해 뜨기 전에)
after	~ 후에	after 5:30 (5시 반 이후에)	after school (수업이 끝난 후에, 방과 후에)
for	~ 동안	for 30 minutes (30분 동안) for two months (두 달 동안)	for an hour (한 시간 동안)

She goes swimming before breakfast. 그녀는 아침 식사 전에 수영을 간다.
They play basketball after school. 그들은 수업이 끝난 후에 농구를 한다.
I sleep for eight hours every day. 나는 매일 8시간 동안 잔다.

for는 주로 시간을 나타내는 숫자와 함께 써요.

STEP 1 기초 탄탄 연습

A 우리말과 같은 뜻이 되도록 빈칸에 알맞은 전치사를 쓰세요.

1. 8시 30분에	________ 8:30	2. 저녁에	________ the evening
3. 토요일에	________ Saturday	4. 9월에	________ September
5. 정오에	________ noon	6. 2023년에	________ 2023
7. 점심을 먹기 전에	________ lunch	8. 30분 동안	________ 30 minutes
9. 가을에	________ fall	10. 해가 진 후에	________ sunset

B 그림을 참고하여 괄호 안에서 알맞은 것을 고르세요.

1.

(on / in) January

2.

(at / in) night

3.

(at / in) the morning

4.

(on / in) winter

5.

(at / in) 2 p.m.

6.

(on / in) August 15th

C 보기의 단어들을 조합하여 우리말에 맞는 표현을 쓰세요.

보기

after	for	before
50 minutes	English class	school

1. 방과 후에 ____________________
2. 50분 동안 ____________________
3. 영어 수업 전에 ____________________

September 9월 sunset 해넘이, 일몰 January 1월 August 8월

STEP 2 규칙 적용 연습

A 그림을 보고 빈칸에 at, on, in 중 알맞은 전치사를 쓰세요.

❶ 
❷ 
❸ 

❹ 

❺ 

1. It is hot and humid __________ summer.

2. Anne's family has dinner __________ 7 p.m.

3. You can visit me __________ Friday.

4. He came to Korea __________ November 2019.

5. I usually read books __________ night.

B 우리말과 같은 뜻이 되도록 괄호 안에서 알맞은 전치사를 고르세요.

1. 나는 보통 아침에 기분이 좋다.
   → I usually feel good (in / on) the morning.

2. 우리 아빠는 해 뜨기 전에 일하러 가신다.
   → My dad goes to work (for / before) sunrise.

3. 그 학생들은 수업이 끝난 후에 간식을 먹는다.
   → The students eat snacks (before / after) class.

4. 그녀는 매일 한 시간 동안 산책을 한다.
   → She takes a walk (for / on) an hour every day.

5. 나는 올해 내 생일에 여행을 갔다.
   → I went on a trip (in / on) my birthday this year.

humid 습한 November 11월 sunrise 해돋이, 일출 snack 간식

C 보기의 전치사 중 알맞은 것과 주어진 표현을 사용하여 우리말에 맞는 문장을 완성하세요.

보기 | at | on | before | for | in

1. 그는 10분 동안 샤워를 한다. (10 minutes)
   → He takes a shower ______________.
2. 그 영화는 오전 11시에 시작했다. (11 a.m.)
   → The movie began ______________
3. 우리는 점심 식사 전에 손을 씻는다. (lunch)
   → We wash our hands ______________.
4. 우리 아빠는 저녁에 운동을 하신다. (the evening)
   → My dad exercises ______________.
5. 우리는 어린이날에 놀이공원에 갔다. (Children's Day)
   → We went to an amusement park ______________.

D ⓐ, ⓑ의 빈칸에 공통으로 들어갈 알맞은 전치사를 쓰세요.

1. ⓐ They don't go to school ________ weekends. 그들은 주말에 학교에 가지 않는다.
   ⓑ I was born ________ March 23rd. 나는 3월 23일에 태어났다.
2. ⓐ I first visited the United States ________ 2020. 나는 2020년에 미국에 처음 방문했다.
   ⓑ My mother does yoga ________ the morning. 우리 엄마는 아침에 요가를 하신다.
3. ⓐ She leaves for school ________ seven thirty. 그녀는 7시 30분에 학교로 출발한다.
   ⓑ My family watches TV ________ night. 우리 가족은 밤에 TV를 본다.
4. ⓐ She studies English ________ an hour every day. 그녀는 매일 1시간 동안 영어를 공부한다.
   ⓑ He usually exercises ________ about an hour. 그는 보통 약 1시간 동안 운동을 한다.

March 3월 do yogo 요가를 하다 leave for ~로 떠나다, 출발하다 about 약, ~쯤

STEP 3 술술 쓰기가 되는 문장 연습

A 우리말 뜻에 맞도록 틀린 부분을 바르게 고쳐 문장을 다시 쓰세요.

1. He was born in December 4th. 그는 12월 4일에 태어났다.
→ ____________________

2. You must not call me at 10 p.m. 밤 10시 이후에는 나한테 전화하면 안 돼.
→ ____________________

3. The store does not open in Tuesdays. 그 상점은 화요일에 문을 열지 않는다.
→ ____________________

4. I usually go to school for breakfast. 나는 보통 아침을 먹은 후에 학교에 간다.
→ ____________________

5. She walks in an hour every day. 그녀는 매일 한 시간 동안 걷는다.
→ ____________________

B 주어진 단어들을 바르게 배열하여 우리말과 같은 뜻이 되도록 문장을 완성하세요.

1. 그 꽃은 봄에 핀다. (in spring / blooms / the flower / .)
→ ____________________

2. 첫 수업은 9시에 시작한다. (class / at 9 / begins / the first / .)
→ ____________________

3. 나는 해가 지기 전에 집에 갔다. (went home / before sunset / I / .)
→ ____________________

4. 우리는 새해 첫날에 산에 갔다. (went / on New Year's Day / we / to the mountain / .)
→ ____________________

5. 나는 매일 2시간 동안 기타를 연습한다.
(for / practice / I / the guitar / every day / two hours / .)
→ ____________________

December 12월 Tuesday 화요일 bloom 꽃이 피다 New Year's Day 1월 1일, 새해 첫날 practice 연습하다

C 방과 후 클럽 활동표를 보고 전치사 at이나 on을 써서 질문에 대한 대답을 완성하세요.

After School Clubs			
Monday	Tuesday	Wednesday	Thursday
Reading 3~4 p.m.	Arts and Crafts 3:30~4:30 p.m.	Baseball 4~5 p.m.	Choir 5~6 p.m.

A: When does the Reading Club meet?

B: They meet ________ Mondays ________ 3 p.m.

A: Does the Arts and Crafts Club meet on Wednesdays?

B: No. They meet ________ Tuesdays.

A: What time does the Choir Club meeting start?

B: It starts ________ 5 p.m.

D 올리비아의 일과표를 보고 알맞은 표현과 보기의 전치사를 사용하여 글을 완성하세요.

7:00 a.m.	get up	7:30 a.m.	have breakfast	8:00 a.m.	go to school	12:00 p.m.	have lunch
4:00 p.m.	play with friends	6:00 p.m.	have dinner	8:00 p.m.	read a book	10:00 p.m.	go to bed

Olivia gets up ________ 7 a.m.

She ________ breakfast ________ going to school.

She ________ ________ ________ noon at school.

She ________ with her friends ________ the afternoon.

She ________ a book ________ dinner.

She ________ ________ bed ________ 10 p.m.

보기
in
at(3번 사용)
before
after

arts and crafts 공예 choir 합창단

UNIT 2 위치, 장소의 전치사

❶ 위치의 전치사

'상자 **안에**', '책상 **아래에**', '학교 **뒤에**', '우체국**과** 빵집 **사이에**'와 같이 위치를 나타낼 때 쓰는 전치사들에는 다음과 같은 것들이 있어요.

in ~ 안에	**on** (붙어서) ~ 위에	**under** ~ 아래에	**near** ~ 가까이에
in front of ~ 앞에	**behind** ~ 뒤에	**next to / beside** ~ 옆에	**between A and B** A와 B 사이에

The cat is in the box. 그 고양이는 상자 안에 있다.
The cat is on the cat tower. 그 고양이는 캣타워 위에 있다.
The cat is under the chair. 그 고양이는 의자 아래에 있다.
The cat is near the pillow. 그 고양이는 베개 가까이에 있다.
The cat is in front of the cat house. 그 고양이는 고양이 집 앞에 있다.
The cat is behind the tree trunk. 그 고양이는 나무 그루터기 뒤에 있다.
The cat is next to the ball. 그 고양이는 공 옆에 있다.
The cat is between the yellow ball and the purple ball.
그 고양이는 노란색 공과 보라색 공 사이에 있다.

❷ 장소의 전치사 in, at

in과 at은 장소를 나타내는 명사 앞에서 '~에서'라는 뜻으로 쓰여요. in은 비교적 넓은 장소 앞에 쓰고, at은 비교적 좁은 장소 앞에 써요.

Jimin lives in Seoul. 지민이는 서울에 산다.
I usually eat dinner at home.
나는 보통 집에서 저녁을 먹는다.

in ~에서 (비교적 넓은 장소)
in Europe (유럽에(서)) **in** Korea (한국에(서))
in this city (이 도시에(서))

at ~에서 (비교적 좁은 장소)
at home (집에(서)) **at** school (학교에(서))
at the bus stop (버스 정류장에(서))

in에는 '~ 안에'라는 뜻이 있어서, 방이나 교실 등 실내 '(안)에서'라는 의미로 in을 써요.
The girl is in her room.

STEP 1 기초 탄탄 연습

A 우리말과 같은 뜻이 되도록 빈칸에 알맞은 전치사를 쓰세요.

1. 방 안에 ________ the room
2. 식탁 아래에 ________ the table
3. 책상 위에 ________ the desk
4. 그 집 앞에 ________ the house
5. 그 건물 옆에 ________ the building
6. 그 건물 뒤에 ________ the building
7. 그 학교 근처에 ________ the school
8. 벤과 팀 사이에 ________ Ben and Tim

B 그림을 보고 알맞은 표현을 골라 √ 표시 하세요.

1.
- ☐ on the sofa
- ☐ under the sofa

2.
- ☐ between the tree
- ☐ beside the tree

3.
- ☐ on the desk
- ☐ under the desk

4.
- ☐ behind the teddy bear
- ☐ between the teddy bear

C 우리말 뜻을 참고하여 괄호 안에서 알맞은 전치사를 고르세요.

1. Indonesia is (at / in) Asia. 인도네시아는 아시아에 있다.
2. They have lunch (at / in) school. 그들은 학교에서 점심을 먹는다.
3. The man lives (at / in) California. 그 남자는 캘리포니아에 산다.
4. I waited for her (at / in) the bus stop. 나는 버스 정류장에서 그녀를 기다렸다.
5. This is the largest stadium (at / in) this city. 이것은 이 도시에서 가장 큰 경기장이다.

building 건물 Indonesia 인도네시아 largest 가장 큰 stadium 경기장

STEP 2 규칙 적용 연습

A 우리말과 같은 뜻이 되도록 괄호 안에서 알맞은 전치사를 고르세요.

1. 나의 강아지는 침대 위에서 자고 있다.
   → My dog is sleeping (on / under) the bed.

2. 우리 집 근처에 시장이 있다.
   → There is a market (behind / near) my house.

3. 그 대학 앞에 지하철역이 있다.
   → There is a subway station (between / in front of) the college.

4. 그는 오늘 학교에서 숙제를 했다.
   → He did his homework (at / on) school today.

5. 그의 집 뒤에 산이 있다.
   → There is a mountain (under / behind) his house.

B 그림을 보고 빈칸에 알맞은 전치사를 쓰세요.

① 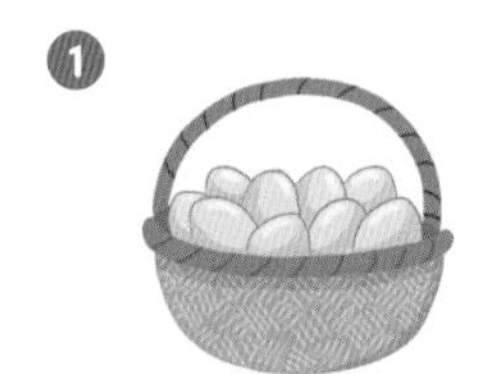

② 

③ 

④ 

⑤ 

1. There are many eggs ____________ the basket.
2. There is a flower vase ____________ the table.
3. A flower shop is ____________ ____________ the bank.
4. Daisy is sitting ____________ her mom and dad.
5. There is a bicycle ____________ front ____________ the house.

 vase 꽃병

C 빈칸에 전치사 in이나 at을 써서 문장을 완성하세요.

1. Did you meet him ___________ the bus stop?
   너는 버스 정류장에서 그를 만났니?

2. This is the tallest building ___________ this city.
   이것은 이 도시에서 가장 높은 건물이다.

3. She is doing her homework ___________ home.
   그녀는 집에서 숙제를 하고 있다.

4. I first met the Japanese girl ___________ Europe.
   나는 그 일본인 소녀를 유럽에서 처음 만났다.

5. My dad is cooking dinner ___________ the kitchen.
   우리 아빠는 주방에서 저녁을 만들고 계신다.

6. Philip and his mother were ___________ New Zealand last year.
   필립과 그의 어머니는 작년에 뉴질랜드에 있었다.

D 보기의 전치사들 중 알맞은 것과 주어진 표현을 사용하여 우리말에 맞는 문장을 완성하세요.

보기	in	behind	near	in front of	under

1. The gallery is ___________________________. (the river)
   그 미술관은 강 근처에 있다.

2. My smartphone was ___________________________. (the room)
   내 스마트폰은 방 안에 있었다.

3. There is a bench ___________________________. (the tree)
   나무 밑에 벤치가 하나 있다.

4. She was sitting ___________________________ in the classroom. (him)
   그녀는 교실에서 그의 뒤에 앉아 있었다.

5. A boy is standing ___________________________. (the library)
   한 남자아이가 도서관 앞에 서 있다.

tallest 가장 높은 Japanese 일본의, 일본인의; 일본인, 일본어 gallery 미술관, 화랑 river 강 stand 서 있다

STEP 3 술술 쓰기가 되는 문장 연습

A 우리말 뜻에 맞도록 틀린 부분을 바르게 고쳐 문장을 다시 쓰세요.

1. The doll was behind her bed. 그 인형은 그녀의 침대 위에 있었다.
→

2. He studied English at Canada. 그는 캐나다에서 영어를 공부했다.
→

3. The bank is next from the hospital. 은행은 병원 옆에 있다.
→

4. A Christmas tree is in front for the building. 그 건물 앞에 크리스마스트리가 있다.
→

5. The Pacific Ocean is between Asia to America. 태평양은 아시아와 아메리카 사이에 있다.
→

B 주어진 단어들을 바르게 배열하여 우리말과 같은 뜻이 되도록 문장을 완성하세요.

1. 나는 2017년에 그 도시에 살았다. (in 2017 / I / lived / the city / in / .)
→

2. 새 한 마리가 우체통 위에 앉아 있다. (the mailbox / a bird / on / is sitting / .)
→

3. 나무 밑에 검은 개가 한 마리 있다. (a black dog / there / under / is / the tree / .)
→

4. 그 남자아이는 내 옆에서 만화책을 읽고 있다.
(the boy / beside / is reading / me / a comic book / .)
→

5. 그의 가게는 커피숍과 약국 사이에 있다.
(his store / a coffee shop / is / and / a drugstore / between / .)
→

the Pacific Ocean 태평양 ocean 대양, 바다 mailbox 우체통 drugstore 약국

C 마을 지도를 보고 빈칸에 알맞은 전치사를 써서 글을 완성하세요.

There is a park and a swimming pool __________ my town.

The park is __________ to a coffee shop.

The library is ____________ the bank __________ the museum.

The department store is __________ the cinema.

The school is __________ the swimming pool.

D 거실 그림을 보고 알맞은 전치사를 넣어 글을 완성하세요.

A table is ______ __________ ______ the sofa.

A bookshelf is __________ the sofa.

A cat is __________ the table.

The sofa is ____________ the table ________ the bookshelf.

The family is ______ the sofa.

department store 백화점 cinema 영화관 bookshelf 책꽂이, 책장

실전 테스트

1-4 빈칸에 알맞은 전치사를 보기에서 골라 번호를 쓰세요.

보기
① in ② before ③ on
④ next to ⑤ at ⑥ for

1
I usually get up ________ 7 a.m.

2
She takes piano lessons ________ Wednesdays.

* take piano lessons 피아노 교습을 받다

3
You should brush your teeth ________ bed.

4
There is a bed ________ the desk.

5-7 우리말과 같은 뜻이 되도록 빈칸에 알맞은 전치사를 고르세요.

5
나의 개는 지금 내 옆에 누워 있다.
My dog is lying ________ me now.

① under ② on
③ between ④ behind
⑤ beside

6
조니는 그의 생일에 파티를 한다.
Johnny has a party ________ his birthday.

① in ② on
③ for ④ after
⑤ before

7
그녀는 매일 30분 동안 달린다.
She runs ________ 30 minutes every day.

① after ② on
③ at ④ for
⑤ from

8-9 빈칸에 공통으로 들어갈 전치사를 고르세요.

8

- They will travel to Vietnam ________ December.
- I first met him ________ London.

① in ② on ③ at
④ for ⑤ from

* Vietnam 베트남

9

- They usually have lunch ________ school.
- I sometimes go for a walk ________ night.

① in ② at ③ to
④ before ⑤ after

10 다음 문장의 해석으로 가장 알맞은 것을 고르세요.

He is sitting behind Jun and Min.

① 그는 준과 민 옆에 앉아 있다.
② 그는 준과 민 근처에 앉아 있다.
③ 그는 준과 민 앞에 앉아 있다.
④ 그는 준과 민 뒤에 앉아 있다.
⑤ 그는 준과 민 사이에 앉아 있다.

11-12 우리말을 영어로 바르게 옮긴 것을 고르세요.

11

미국은 캐나다와 멕시코 사이에 있다.

① The United States is near Canada and Mexico.
② The United States is next to Canada and Mexico.
③ The United States is between Canada and Mexico.
④ The United States is behind Canada and Mexico.
⑤ The United States is in Canada and Mexico.

12

그녀는 4월 17일에 태어났다.

① She was born in April 17th.
② She was born in April on 17th.
③ She was born at April 17th.
④ She was born on April 17th.
⑤ She was born from April 17th.

13 밑줄 친 부분이 틀린 문장을 고르세요.

① The city is beautiful in autumn.
② He came home at 3 today.
③ They have lunch at noon.
④ The boy band is popular in the U.S.
⑤ I watched the movie in home.

14 우리말을 참고하여 빈칸에 들어갈 말이 바르게 짝지어진 것을 고르세요.

- The church was ________ front of a library.
  그 교회는 도서관 앞에 있었다.
- Their house is ________ the park.
  그들의 집은 그 공원 근처에 있다.

① in - near ② on - near
③ to - under ④ in - next
⑤ on - between

15 다음 문장을 바르게 고치는 방법으로 알맞은 것을 고르세요.

They take a walk on the evening.

① take를 takes로 고친다.
② take를 did not took으로 고친다.
③ on the evening을 in the evening으로 고친다.
④ on the evening을 at the evening으로 고친다.
⑤ on the evening을 at evening으로 고친다.

16-17 밑줄 친 부분을 바르게 고친 것으로 짝지어진 것을 고르세요.

16
- They exercise at the morning.
- The boys play basketball in Saturday.

① in - on ② in - at
③ on - on ④ in - for
⑤ on - by

17
- Jin was born and lives at Seoul.
- She is sleeping in home now.

① in - on ② on - at
③ in - at ④ in - by
⑤ from - at

18-19 우리말과 같은 뜻이 되도록 빈칸에 알맞은 전치사를 쓰세요.

18
나는 점심을 먹고 나서 산책을 한다.
→ I take a walk ________ lunch.

19
그녀는 그를 한 시간 동안 기다렸다.
→ She waited for him ________ an hour.

20-21 빈칸에 공통으로 들어갈 전치사를 쓰세요.

20
• Kate went to London ________ July.
• They are talking ________ the classroom.

21
• I usually get up ________ seven thirty a.m.
• She met her friend ________ the bus stop.

22-23 우리말 뜻에 맞도록 틀린 부분을 바르게 고쳐 문장을 다시 쓰세요.

22
There is a bike on front of his house.
그의 집 앞에 자전거가 한 대 있다.
→ ________________________
____

23
You should not go out for night.
밤에 외출하지 않는 게 좋아요.
→ ________________________
____

24-25 주어진 단어들을 바르게 배열하여 우리말과 같은 뜻이 되도록 문장을 완성하세요.

24
나는 2018년에 그 영화를 보았다.
(saw / in 2018 / I / the movie / .)
→ ________________________
____

25
그 슈퍼마켓은 빵집 근처에 있다.
(is / the bakery / the supermarket / near / .)
→ ________________________
____

Word List Chapter 6

앞에서 배운 단어를 한 번 더 확인하고 어렵거나 모르는 단어는 다시 공부하세요.

☐	about	약, ~쯤	☐	August	8월
☐	behind	~ 뒤에	☐	beside	~ 옆에
☐	bloom	꽃이 피다	☐	bookshelf	책꽂이, 책장
☐	building	건물	☐	choir	합창단
☐	cinema	영화관	☐	dawn	새벽
☐	December	12월	☐	department store	백화점
☐	drugstore	약국	☐	February	2월
☐	gallery	미술관, 화랑	☐	humid	습한
☐	January	1월	☐	Japanese	일본(인)의; 일본인, 일본어
☐	leave	떠나다, 출발하다	☐	mailbox	우체통
☐	March	3월	☐	midnight	자정, 밤 12시
☐	minute	분	☐	near	~ 가까이에
☐	noon	정오, 낮 12시	☐	November	11월
☐	ocean	대양, 바다	☐	practice	연습하다
☐	river	강	☐	September	9월
☐	snack	간식	☐	stadium	경기장
☐	stand	서 있다	☐	sunrise	해돋이, 일출
☐	sunset	해넘이, 일몰	☐	vase	꽃병

기적의 초등 영문법 2

UNIT 1 현재진행형

A 다음 영어 단어에는 우리말 뜻을 쓰고, 우리말 뜻에는 영어 단어를 쓰세요.

	단어	우리말 뜻		우리말 뜻	단어
1	bake		16	쓰다	
2	cut		17	씻다	
3	lie		18	~를 기다리다	
4	move		19	말하다, 이야기하다	
5	put		20	수영하다	
6	read		21	자다	
7	ride		22	노래하다	
8	run		23	달리다	
9	sing		24	(탈것을) 타다	
10	sleep		25	읽다	
11	swim		26	놓다, 두다	
12	talk		27	옮기다, 움직이다	
13	wait for		28	눕다	
14	wash		29	자르다	
15	write		30	굽다	

B POINT를 참고하여 둘 중 알맞은 것을 골라 빈칸에 넣어 현재진행형 문장을 완성하세요.

POINT

- I **am eating** breakfast now. She **is reading** a book.

현재진행형은 <be동사+동사ing> 형태로, '~하고 있다, ~하는 중이다'라는 뜻이다.

- He **is driving** a truck. | 동사의 -ing형을 만들 때 <자음+-e>로 끝나는 동사는 e를 빼고 -ing를 붙인다.

1. I am ______________ my homework. ☐ do ☐ doing
   나는 숙제를 하고 있다.
2. David is ______________ now. ☐ comes ☐ coming
   데이비드는 지금 오고 있다.
3. He is ______________ a paper ship. ☐ making ☐ makeing
   그는 종이배를 만들고 있다.
4. My grandma is ______________ TV. ☐ watcheing ☐ watching
   우리 할머니는 TV를 보고 계신다.
5. My cat is ______________ now. ☐ sleeps ☐ sleeping
   나의 고양이는 지금 자고 있다.
6. Jimmy is ______________ a bike. ☐ riding ☐ rideing
   지미는 자전거를 타고 있다.

C POINT를 참고하여 주어진 동사를 사용하여 현재진행형 문장을 완성하세요.

POINT

- The cat **is lying** on the floor. | -ie로 끝나는 동사는 ie를 y로 바꾸고 -ing를 붙인다.
- The boy **is running** with his dog.

<모음 1+자음 1>로 끝나는 동사는 자음을 한 번 더 쓰고 -ing를 붙인다.

1. She ______________ now. (run) 그녀는 지금 달리고 있다.
2. They ______________ on the bench. (sit) 그들은 벤치에 앉아 있다.
3. The girl ______________ paper. (cut) 그 여자아이는 종이를 자르고 있다.
4. The boys ______________ in the sea. (swim) 그 남자아이들은 바다에서 수영하고 있다.
5. The man ______________ on the sofa. (lie) 그 남자는 소파에 누워 있다.
6. He ______________ around the house. (run) 그는 집 안을 뛰어다니고 있다.

D 우리말과 같은 뜻이 되도록 주어진 동사를 알맞은 형태로 빈칸에 쓰세요.

1. 나는 지금 프렌치토스트를 먹고 있다.
   → I ________________ French toast now. (eat)

2. 그들은 축구를 하고 있다.
   → They ________________ soccer. (play)

3. 그녀는 일기를 쓰고 있다.
   → She ________________ in her diary. (write)

4. 우리는 풀밭에 누워 있다.
   → We ________________ on the grass. (lie)

5. 우리 아빠는 차를 운전하고 계신다.
   → My dad ________________ his car. (drive)

6. 나는 지금 핫초콜릿을 마시고 있다.
   → I ________________ hot chocolate now. (drink)

E 우리말 뜻을 참고하여 밑줄 친 부분을 바르게 고치세요.

1. I is washing my hands now. → ________________
   나는 지금 손을 씻고 있다.

2. The man is take pictures of children. → ________________
   그 남자는 아이들의 사진을 찍고 있다.

3. Annie is readding a novel. → ________________
   애니는 소설을 읽고 있다.

4. We are watch a comedy movie. → ________________
   우리는 코미디 영화를 보고 있다.

5. My mom is bakeing bread. → ________________
   우리 엄마는 빵을 굽고 계신다.

6. The students are studing English. → ________________
   그 학생들은 영어를 공부하고 있다.

Challenge!

F

주어진 단어들을 사용하여 우리말과 같은 뜻의 현재진행형 영어 문장을 쓰세요. (필요한 단어들을 추가하세요.)

1. 우리는 그림을 그리고 있다. (draw, pictures)

→ ______________________________

2. 나는 엄마를 기다리고 있다. (wait, for my mom)

→ ______________________________

3. 새들은 하늘을 날고 있다. (the birds, fly, in the sky)

→ ______________________________

4. 그 작가는 소설을 쓰고 있다. (the writer, write, a novel)

→ ______________________________

5. 말들이 들판에서 달리고 있다. (the horses, run, in the field)

→ ______________________________

6. 나는 지금 내 방을 청소하고 있다. (clean, my room, now)

→ ______________________________

7. 제임스는 소파에서 자고 있다. (James, sleep, on the sofa)

→ ______________________________

8. 그녀는 강아지와 함께 산책하고 있다. (take, a walk, with her dog)

→ ______________________________

9. 그 어린 소녀는 양치질을 하고 있다. (the little girl, brush, her teeth)

→ ______________________________

10. 그 소년은 한 할머니를 도와드리고 있다. (the boy, help, an old woman)

→ ______________________________

현재진행형의 부정문과 의문문

A 다음 영어 단어에는 우리말 뜻을 쓰고, 우리말 뜻에는 영어 단어를 쓰세요.

	단어	우리말 뜻		우리말 뜻	단어
1	beside		16	가르치다	
2	classroom		17	거리	
3	clean		18	딸기	
4	cook		19	운동장, 놀이터	
5	cry		20	(귀 기울여) 듣다	
6	drink		21	도서관	
7	floor		22	배우다	
8	laugh		23	웃다	
9	learn		24	바닥	
10	library		25	마시다	
11	listen		26	울다	
12	playground		27	요리하다; 요리사	
13	strawberry		28	청소하다	
14	street		29	교실	
15	teach		30	~ 옆에	

B POINT를 참고하여 현재진행형 문장을 부정문으로 바꿔 문장을 완성하세요.

POINT

- I **am not sleeping**. She **is not writing** a letter.
  They **are not watching** TV.

현재진행형의 부정문은 be동사 뒤에 not을 쓴다. '~하고 있지 않다'라는 뜻이다.

1. I am reading a book. 나는 책을 읽고 있다.
   부정문 I ______________________ a book.
2. You are washing the dishes. 너는 설거지를 하고 있다.
   부정문 You ______________________ the dishes.
3. It is snowing outside. 밖에 눈이 오고 있다.
   부정문 It ______________________ outside.
4. We are eating dinner now. 우리는 지금 저녁을 먹고 있다.
   부정문 We ______________________ dinner now.
5. The dog is playing with a toy. 그 개는 장난감을 갖고 놀고 있다.
   부정문 The dog ______________________ with a toy.

C POINT를 참고하여 괄호 안에서 알맞은 표현을 고르세요.

POINT

- **Are** you **doing** your homework? **Is** it **raining** outside?
  Are the kids **playing** mobile games?

현재진행형의 의문문은 be동사를 문장 맨 앞으로 보내서 <be동사+주어+동사ing ~?> 어순으로 쓴다.
'~하고 있어요?, ~하는 중이에요?'라고, 말하는 순간 어떤 행동을 하고 있는지 묻는다.

1. Is the baby (cry / crying)? 그 아기가 울고 있나요?
2. Are you (talk / talking) on the phone? 너 통화 중이니?
3. (Do they singing / Are they singing) songs? 그들은 노래를 부르고 있나요?
4. (Are / Is) the man driving a bus? 그 남자는 버스를 운전하고 있나요?
5. (Does she take / Is she taking) a walk now? 그녀는 지금 산책을 하고 있나요?

D POINT를 참고하여 질문에 알맞은 대답을 완성하세요.

POINT

- **Are** you **doing** your homework? ----- **Yes**, I **am**. / **No**, I'**m not**.
  Is it **raining** outside? ----- **Yes**, it **is**. / **No**, it **isn't**.
  Are the kids **playing** baseball? ----- **Yes**, they **are**. / **No**, they **aren't**.

현재진행형의 의문문에 대한 대답은 긍정이면 Yes, 부정이면 No로 한다.

1. Are you studying English? ----- No, ______________.
   너 영어 공부하고 있니?
2. Is your dad watching TV? ----- Yes, ______________.
   너희 아빠는 TV를 보고 계시니?
3. Is she listening to the radio? ----- No, ______________.
   그녀는 라디오를 듣고 있나요?
4. Are they playing a board game? ----- No, ______________.
   그들은 보드게임을 하고 있나요?
5. Is your mom watering the plants? ----- Yes, ______________.
   너희 엄마는 식물에 물을 주고 계시니?

E 우리말 뜻을 참고하여 틀린 부분을 찾아 바르게 고치세요.

1. She does not cooking dinner. 그녀는 저녁을 요리하고 있지 않다.
   ______________ → ______________
2. The boy not playing the piano. 그 남자아이는 피아노를 치고 있지 않다.
   ______________ → ______________
3. Are you wash your face now? 너 지금 세수하고 있니?
   ______________ → ______________
4. Does she eating strawberries? 그녀가 딸기를 먹고 있나요?
   ______________ → ______________
5. They are not runing in the classroom. 그들은 교실에서 뛰고 있지 않다.
   ______________ → ______________

F 각 문장을 지시대로 다시 쓰세요.

1. The cat is drinking water. 그 고양이는 물을 마시고 있다.

부정문 ______________________________

2. Bill and Jessica are playing tennis. 빌과 제시카는 테니스를 치고 있다.

부정문 ______________________________

3. You are eating breakfast. 너는 아침을 먹고 있다.

의문문 ______________________________

4. The woman is lying on the couch. 그 여성은 소파에 누워 있다.

의문문 ______________________________

5. The dog is barking at the man. 그 개가 그 남자를 보고 짖고 있다.

의문문 ______________________________

Challenge! G 주어진 단어들을 사용하여 우리말과 같은 뜻의 현재진행형 영어 문장을 쓰세요. (필요한 단어들을 추가하세요.)

1. 제니는 빗속을 걷고 있지 않다. (Jenny, walk, in the rain)

→ ______________________________

2. 우리는 지금 배구를 하고 있지 않다. (play, volleyball, now)

→ ______________________________

3. 너는 잡지를 읽고 있니? (read, a magazine)

→ ______________________________

4. 그는 유튜브를 보고 있나요? (watch, YouTube)

→ ______________________________

5. 그들은 영어를 배우고 있나요? (learn, English)

→ ______________________________

UNIT 1 can

A 다음 영어 단어에는 우리말 뜻을 쓰고, 우리말 뜻에는 영어 단어를 쓰세요.

	단어	우리말 뜻		우리말 뜻	단어
1	baseball		16	단어	
2	basketball		17	채소	
3	build		18	이해하다	
4	carry		19	오늘 밤에; 오늘 밤	
5	enter		20	시험	
6	fix		21	풀다, 해결하다	
7	help		22	문제	
8	pass		23	통과하다	
9	problem		24	돕다	
10	solve		25	고치다, 수리하다	
11	test		26	들어가다	
12	tonight		27	들다, 운반하다	
13	understand		28	짓다, 세우다	
14	vegetable		29	농구	
15	word		30	야구	

B POINT를 참고하여 우리말 뜻에 맞도록 괄호 안에서 알맞은 것을 고르세요.

POINT

- I **can speak** English. 조동사 can은 '~할 수 있다'라는 뜻이다. can 뒤에는 동사원형이 온다.
- I **can't speak** English.

'~할 수 없다'라는 부정의 의미는 <cannot+동사원형>으로 나타낸다. cannot은 보통 줄여서 can't로 쓴다.

1. I can (sing / singing) the song. 나는 그 노래를 부를 수 있다.
2. John can (makes / make) a sandwich. 존은 샌드위치를 만들 수 있다.
3. She cannot (play / plays) tennis. 그녀는 테니스를 치지 못한다.
4. Penguins (can / can't) fly. 펭귄들은 날지 못한다.
5. They (can / can't) speak Chinese. 그들은 중국어를 할 줄 안다.
6. He (can / can't) read English books. 그는 영어로 된 책을 읽지 못한다.

C POINT를 참고하여 괄호 안에서 알맞은 것을 고르세요.

POINT

- **Can** you **speak** English? ----- **Yes,** I **can.** / **No,** I **can't.**
  Can he **swim**? ----- **Yes,** he **can.** / **No,** he **can't.**

'~할 수 있어요?'라고 물어보는 의문문은 조동사 can을 주어 앞으로 보내서 <Can+주어+동사원형 ~?>으로 쓴다.
긍정 대답은 Yes로, 부정 대답은 No로 한다.

1. Can you (riding / ride) a bike? 너 자전거 탈 수 있어?
2. Can she (go / goes) there alone? 그녀는 거기 혼자 갈 수 있나요?
3. Can the boy (run / runs) fast? 그 남자아이는 빨리 달릴 수 있나요?
4. Can they (play / played) basketball? 그들은 농구를 할 줄 아나요?
5. Can (cook you / you cook) bulgogi? 너는 불고기를 요리할 수 있니?
6. (Do they can / Can they) swim? 그들은 수영을 할 줄 아나요?
7. Can (write you / you write) in English? 너는 영어로 글을 쓸 수 있니?
8. (Does he can / Can he) bake bread? 그는 빵을 구울 줄 아나요?

D 질문에 알맞은 대답을 완성하세요.

1. Can they ski? ----- Yes, ______________.
2. Can you get up early? ----- No, ______________.
3. Can it jump high? ----- Yes, ______________.
4. Can the baby girl walk? ----- No, ______________.

E 우리말과 같은 뜻이 되도록 빈칸에 주어진 동사와 알맞은 조동사를 쓰세요.

1. 나는 내일 파티에 갈 수 있다.
   → I ________ ________ to the party tomorrow. (go)
2. 너는 파스타를 요리할 수 있니?
   → ________ you ________ pasta? (cook)
3. 그 남자아이는 채소를 먹지 못한다.
   → The boy ________ ________ vegetables. (eat)
4. 너희 할아버지는 스마트폰을 사용하실 수 있니?
   → ________ your grandfather ________ a smartphone? (use)

F 우리말 뜻을 참고하여 틀린 부분을 찾아 바르게 고치세요.

1. Tim can plays the piano well. 팀은 피아노를 잘 친다.
   ______________ → ______________
2. Can wash you the dishes now? 너 지금 설거지할 수 있니?
   ______________ → ______________
3. The child doesn't can speak Korean. 그 아이는 한국어를 하지 못한다.
   ______________ → ______________
4. We can skate not outside in summer. 우리는 여름에 밖에서 스케이트를 타지 못한다.
   ______________ → ______________

G 각 문장을 지시대로 다시 쓰세요.

1. I can drink cold water.

부정문 ______________________

2. She can swim well.

의문문 ______________________

3. The old man can walk.

부정문 ______________________

4. The cat can open the door.

의문문 ______________________

5. Yumin can solve the problem.

부정문 ______________________

Challenge! H 주어진 단어들과 알맞은 조동사를 사용하여 우리말과 같은 뜻의 영어 문장을 쓰세요. (필요한 단어들을 추가하세요.)

1. 나는 그것을 이해할 수 있다. (understand, it)

→ ______________________

2. 톰은 운전을 하지 못한다. (Tom, drive, a car)

→ ______________________

3. 너 김치 먹을 수 있어? (eat, kimchi)

→ ______________________

4. 그 아이는 자전거를 타지 못한다. (the child, ride, a bicycle)

→ ______________________

5. 그녀는 바이올린을 연주할 수 있나요? (play, the violin)

→ ______________________

UNIT 2 must와 have to

A 다음 영어 단어에는 우리말 뜻을 쓰고, 우리말 뜻에는 영어 단어를 쓰세요.

	단어	우리말 뜻		우리말 뜻	단어
1	bring		16	우산	
2	call		17	아끼다, 모으다	
3	cross		18	도로, 길	
4	exam		19	돌려주다	
5	exercise		20	~에 대답하다, 답장을 보내다	
6	feed		21	약속	
7	keep		22	박물관, 미술관	
8	lock		23	잠그다	
9	museum		24	~한 상태로 유지하다	
10	promise		25	먹이를 주다	
11	reply to		26	운동하다	
12	return		27	시험	
13	road		28	건너다, 횡단하다	
14	save		29	전화하다	
15	umbrella		30	데려오다, 가져오다	

B POINT를 참고하여 괄호 안에서 알맞은 것을 고르세요.

POINT

- I **must do** my homework tonight.
  He **must do** his homework tonight.
  조동사 must는 '반드시 ~해야 한다'라는 뜻이다. 뒤에는 동사원형이 온다.
- I **have to do** my homework tonight.
  She **has to do** her homework tonight.
  have to는 must와 같은 뜻이다. 단, 주어가 3인칭 단수일 때는 has to로 쓴다.

1. I (must / must to) get up at 6 tomorrow. 나는 내일 6시에 일어나야 한다.
2. John (have to / has to) call his mom. 존은 엄마에게 전화를 해야 한다.
3. You (must / must to) wash your hands. 너는 손을 씻어야 한다.
4. Elizabeth must (go / goes) home now. 엘리자베스는 지금 집에 가야 한다.
5. We (must to / have to) clean our classroom. 우리는 교실을 청소해야 한다.
6. She (have to / has to) read the book. 그녀는 그 책을 읽어야 한다.
7. They (have to / has to) take the bus. 그들은 그 버스를 타야 한다.

C POINT를 참고하여 우리말 뜻에 맞게 괄호 안에서 알맞은 것을 고르세요.

POINT

- You **must not touch** this. must의 부정 표현인 must not은 '~하면 안 된다'라는 뜻이다.
- You **don't have to clean** the room. He **doesn't have to come** today.
  have to의 부정 표현인 'don't[doesn't] have to'는 '~할 필요 없다, ~하지 않아도 된다'라는 뜻이다.

1. You (must not / have to) eat the bread. 너는 그 빵을 먹으면 안 된다.
2. We (have no to / don't have to) do the work. 우리는 그 일을 하지 않아도 된다.
3. She (doesn't have to / must not) watch TV now. 그녀는 지금 TV를 보면 안 된다.
4. You (don't have to / don't must) close the door. 문 안 닫아도 돼요.
5. They (don't have to / must not) go there today. 그들은 오늘 거기 안 가도 된다.
6. You (have not to / must not) turn on the light. 불 켜면 안 돼요.
7. I (must not / don't have to) wash my hair today. 나는 오늘 머리를 안 감아도 된다.

D 우리말과 같은 뜻이 되도록 괄호 안에서 알맞은 것을 고르세요.

1. 너는 창문을 닫아야 한다.
   → You (must / must not) close the window.
2. 그는 그 질문에 답해야 한다.
   → He (have to / has to) answer the question.
3. 그 아이는 지금 길을 건너야 한다.
   → The child (must / must not) cross the street now.
4. 그녀는 그를 기다리지 않아도 된다.
   → She (has to / doesn't have to) wait for him.
5. 꽃밭에 들어가면 안 된다.
   → You (must / must not) go into the flower garden.
6. 나는 지금 답을 확인하지 않아도 된다.
   → I (must not / don't have to) check the answers now.
7. 여기서 큰 소리로 이야기하면 안 됩니다.
   → You (must not / don't have to) talk loudly here.

E 우리말 뜻을 참고하여 틀린 부분을 찾아 바르게 고치세요.

1. She have to write an email. 그녀는 이메일을 한 통 써야 한다.
   ______________ → ______________
2. You must keeps your promise. 너는 약속을 지켜야 한다.
   ______________ → ______________
3. I don't have cook dinner today. 나는 오늘 저녁을 요리하지 않아도 된다.
   ______________ → ______________
4. They must not are late for school. 그들은 학교에 늦으면 안 된다.
   ______________ → ______________
5. You must play the piano late at night. 너는 밤 늦게 피아노를 치면 안 된다.
   ______________ → ______________

Challenge!

F 주어진 단어들과 알맞은 조동사를 사용하여 우리말과 같은 뜻의 영어 문장을 쓰세요. (필요한 단어들을 추가하세요.)

1. 나는 돈을 모아야 한다. (save, money)

→ ______________________________

2. 그녀는 치과에 가야 한다. (go to the dentist)

→ ______________________________

3. 나는 오늘 집 청소를 안 해도 된다. (clean, the house, today)

→ ______________________________

4. 사탕을 너무 많이 먹으면 안 된다. (you, eat, too much candy)

→ ______________________________

5. 우리 아빠는 내일 출근하셔야 한다. (my dad, go to work, tomorrow)

→ ______________________________

6. 우리는 오늘 도시락을 싸지 않아도 된다. (pack, our lunch, today)

→ ______________________________

7. 거기서는 사진을 찍으면 안 됩니다. (you, take pictures, there)

→ ______________________________

8. 그는 새 노트북을 사야 한다. (buy, a new laptop computer)

→ ______________________________

9. 나는 금요일에 교복을 입지 않아도 된다. (wear, a school uniform, on Fridays)

→ ______________________________

10. 그들은 내일 기차역에 일찍 도착해야 한다. (arrive, at the train station, early tomorrow)

→ ______________________________

UNIT 3 may와 should

A 다음 영어 단어에는 우리말 뜻을 쓰고, 우리말 뜻에는 영어 단어를 쓰세요.

	단어	우리말 뜻		우리말 뜻	단어
1	aloud		16	사용하다	
2	also		17	만지다, 손대다	
3	breakfast		18	머무르다, 계속 있다	
4	coat		19	(돈을) 지불하다	
5	doll		20	그림	
6	each other		21	떠나다	
7	event		22	건강에 좋은	
8	grass		23	잔디밭, 풀	
9	healthy		24	사건, 일, 행사	
10	leave		25	서로	
11	painting		26	인형	
12	pay		27	외투	
13	stay		28	아침 식사	
14	touch		29	또한, 게다가	
15	use		30	소리 내어, 큰 소리로	

B POINT를 참고하여 우리말 뜻에 맞게 괄호 안에서 알맞은 것을 고르세요.

POINT

- You **may come** in. | 조동사 may는 '~해도 된다'라는 뜻이다. 뒤에는 동사원형이 온다.
- You **may not go** out after 10 p.m.

부정형 may not은 '~하면 안 된다'라는 의미로, must not(절대로 ~하면 안 된다)보다 약하게 금지하는 느낌이다.

1. You may (eat / to eat) this. 이거 먹어도 돼.
2. She may (goes / go) to bed now. 그녀는 지금 자도 된다.
3. He (may / may not) go out now. 그는 지금 외출하면 안 된다.
4. We may (go / going) home now. 우리는 지금 집에 가도 된다.
5. They (may not / don't have to) enter the room. 그들은 그 방에 들어가면 안 된다.
6. You (may do use / may use) this computer. 너는 이 컴퓨터를 사용해도 된다.
7. You (may not eat / don't may eat) on the subway.
지하철에서는 음식을 먹으면 안 된다.

C POINT를 참고하여 괄호 안에서 알맞은 것을 고르세요.

POINT

- **May** I **come** in? ----- **Yes**, you **may**. / **No**, you **may not**.

'~해도 될까요?'라고 허락을 구하는 의문문은 may를 주어 앞으로 보내서 <May+주어+동사원형 ~?>으로 쓴다.
대답은 Yes와 No를 써서 한다.

1. (May eat I / May I eat) this bread?
이 빵 먹어도 돼요?
2. (May I go / May do I go) to your house now?
지금 너희 집에 가도 될까?
3. (May she goes / May she go) back home now?
그녀가 지금 집에 돌아가도 될까요?
4. May I use your phone? ----- (Yes, I may. / Yes, you may.)
당신 전화기 좀 써도 될까요?
5. May we stay here tonight? ----- (No, you may. / No, you may not.)
우리가 오늘 밤 여기 묵어도 되나요?

D POINT를 참고하여 우리말 뜻에 맞도록 괄호 안에서 알맞은 것을 고르세요.

POINT

- You **should go** to bed early.

  조동사 should는 '~하는 게 좋다, ~해야 한다'라는 뜻으로, '충고'나 '조언'을 나타낸다.

- You **should not go** to bed late.

  부정형인 should not은 '~하지 않는 게 좋다, ~하면 안 된다'라는 뜻이다.

1. You (may / should) do it now. 너는 지금 그걸 하는 게 좋겠어.
2. We (must not / should not) talk about it. 우리는 그 이야기는 하지 않는 게 좋겠어.
3. You (should / can) work out every day. 매일 운동하는 게 좋아요.
4. You (cannot / should not) drink too much soda. 탄산음료를 너무 많이 마시지 않는 게 좋다.
5. They (must / should) leave now. 그들은 지금 출발하는 게 좋겠어.
6. You (don't have to / should not) drive on snowy days.
   눈이 오는 날에는 운전하지 않는 게 좋다.

E 우리말 뜻을 참고하여 틀린 부분을 찾아 바르게 고치세요.

1. You may not drink beverages here. 여기서 음료를 마셔도 됩니다.

   ____________ → ____________

2. You should not brush your teeth every night. 매일 밤 양치질을 하는 게 좋아.

   ____________ → ____________

3. May I invited Mike to my birthday party? 내 생일 파티에 마이크를 초대해도 돼요?

   ____________ → ____________

4. You should not eating too much sugar. 설탕을 너무 많이 먹지 않는 게 좋다.

   ____________ → ____________

5. You may not opens the door of the room. 그 방의 문을 열면 안 돼요.

   ____________ → ____________

Challenge!

F 주어진 단어들과 조동사 may나 should를 사용하여 우리말과 같은 뜻의 영어 문장을 쓰세요. (필요한 단어들을 추가하세요.)

1. 너희는 여기서 놀아도 된다. (play, here)

→ ______________________________

2. 창문 좀 열어도 될까요? (open, the window)

→ ______________________________

3. 아이들은 이 책을 읽으면 안 돼요. (children, should, this book)

→ ______________________________

4. 아침밥을 매일 먹는 게 좋아요. (you, breakfast, every day)

→ ______________________________

5. 여기서 손을 닦으시면 됩니다. (you, wash, your hands, here)

→ ______________________________

6. 제가 질문 하나 해도 될까요? (ask, you, a question)

→ ______________________________

7. 그림들에 손대면 안 됩니다. (you, should, touch, the pictures)

→ ______________________________

8. 너는 여기에 저녁 8시까지 있어도 된다. (stay, here, until 8 p.m.)

→ ______________________________

9. 이 동물들에게 먹이를 주면 안 됩니다. (you, should, feed, these animals)

→ ______________________________

10. 너는 식사 전에 손을 씻어야 한다. (wash, your hands, before eating)

→ ______________________________

UNIT 1 be동사의 과거형

A 다음 영어 단어에는 우리말 뜻을 쓰고, 우리말 뜻에는 영어 단어를 쓰세요.

	단어	우리말 뜻		우리말 뜻	단어
1	again		16	목소리	
2	ago		17	피곤한	
3	basket		18	목이 마른	
4	busy		19	과학	
5	city		20	식당	
6	delicious		21	재미있는	
7	famous		22	정원	
8	fresh		23	신선한	
9	garden		24	유명한	
10	interesting		25	맛있는	
11	restaurant		26	도시	
12	science		27	바쁜	
13	thirsty		28	바구니	
14	tired		29	~ 전에	
15	voice		30	또, 다시	

B POINT를 참고하여 빈칸에 알맞은 be동사의 과거형을 쓰세요.

POINT

- I **was** 11 years old last year. You **were** at home last night.
  He **was** a student in 2015. They **were** in Paris last fall.

be동사의 과거형은 '~였다, (~에) 있었다, (상태가) ~했다'라고 과거의 상태를 나타낸다.
주어가 I, he, she, it, 단수 명사일 때는 was를 쓰고, 주어가 you, we, they, 복수 명사일 때는 were를 쓴다.

1. I ________ at home last Saturday. 나는 지난 토요일에 집에 있었다.
2. We ________ in New York two years ago. 우리는 2년 전에 뉴욕에 있었다.
3. She ________ sick last night. 그녀는 어젯밤에 아팠다.
4. There ________ a tall building here then. 그때는 여기에 높은 건물이 있었다.
5. They ________ at the museum yesterday. 그들은 어제 그 박물관에 있었다.
6. The kids ________ in the library this morning. 그 아이들은 오늘 아침에 도서관에 있었다.
7. Mr. Anderson ________ our English teacher last year.
   앤더슨 선생님은 작년에 우리 영어 선생님이셨다.

C POINT를 참고하여 우리말 뜻에 맞도록 괄호 안에서 알맞은 be동사를 고르세요.

POINT

- It **is** rainy today. be동사의 현재형은 현재의 사실이나 상태를 나타낸다.
- It **was** rainy yesterday. be동사의 과거형은 과거의 사실이나 상태를 나타낸다.

1. I (am / was) very hungry now. 나는 지금 너무 배가 고프다.
2. We (are / were) in the same class in 2019. 우리는 2019년에 같은 반이었다.
3. The woman (is / was) always kind. 그 여성은 항상 친절하다.
4. He (is / was) with his friends last night. 그는 어젯밤에 친구들과 함께 있었다.
5. The children (are / were) in the playground then. 그 아이들은 그때 운동장에 있었다.
6. Tommy and James (are / were) good friends now. 토미와 제임스는 지금 좋은 친구다.
7. The cat (is / was) on the roof this morning. 그 고양이는 오늘 아침에 지붕 위에 있었다.

D 우리말과 같은 뜻이 되도록 빈칸에 알맞은 be동사를 쓰세요.

1. 그 남자는 버스에 있었다.
   → The man ____________ on the bus.
2. 상자 속에 책이 많이 있었다.
   → There ____________ many books in the box.
3. 토머스 에디슨은 유명한 발명가였다.
   → Thomas Edison ____________ a famous inventor.
4. 우리는 그때 초등학생이었다.
   → We ____________ elementary school students then.
5. 존과 그레이스는 작년에 열네 살이었다.
   → John and Grace ____________ 14 years old last year.

E 우리말 뜻을 참고하여 틀린 부분을 찾아 바르게 고치세요.

1. Yesterday is my mother's birthday. 어제는 우리 엄마 생신이었다.
   ____________ → ____________
2. She was in the fourth grade this year. 그녀는 올해 4학년이다.
   ____________ → ____________
3. There is a bridge here at that time. 그때는 여기에 다리가 하나 있었다.
   ____________ → ____________
4. The children were at Charlie's house now. 그 아이들은 지금 찰리의 집에 있다.
   ____________ → ____________
5. They are at their grandmother's house last weekend.
   그들은 지난 주말에 할머니 댁에 있었다.
   ____________ → ____________

Challenge!

F 주어진 단어들과 알맞은 be동사를 사용하여 우리말과 같은 뜻의 영어 문장을 쓰세요. (필요한 단어들을 추가하세요.)

1. 나는 어젯밤에 피곤했다. (tired, last night)

→ ____________________

2. 어제 날씨는 흐렸다. (it, cloudy, yesterday)

→ ____________________

3. 그때 우리는 유치원생이었다. (kindergartners, then)

→ ____________________

4. 그 노부인은 나무 밑에 있었다. (the old lady, under a tree)

→ ____________________

5. 나의 개는 작년에 열두 살이었다. (my dog, old, last year)

→ ____________________

6. 탁자 위에 컵이 4개 있었다. (there, cups, on the table)

→ ____________________

7. 가을 하늘은 높고 파랬다. (the autumn sky, high and blue)

→ ____________________

8. 나의 할아버지는 수학 선생님이셨다. (my grandfather, a math teacher)

→ ____________________

9. 그들은 2020년에 초등학생이었다. (elementary school students, in 2020)

→ ____________________

10. 리나와 그녀의 어머니는 빵집에 있었다. (Lena, her mother, at a bakery)

→ ____________________

UNIT 2 be동사 과거형의 부정문과 의문문

A 다음 영어 단어에는 우리말 뜻을 쓰고, 우리말 뜻에는 영어 단어를 쓰세요.

	단어	우리말 뜻		우리말 뜻	단어
1	aunt		16	방학	
2	autumn		17	놀란	
3	bakery		18	아픈	
4	balloon		19	신발	
5	difficult		20	슬픈	
6	expensive		21	둥근	
7	purple		22	반지	
8	rainy		23	비가 오는	
9	ring		24	보라색의; 보라색	
10	round		25	비싼	
11	sad		26	어려운	
12	shoes		27	풍선	
13	sick		28	빵집	
14	surprised		29	가을	
15	vacation		30	이모, 고모, 숙모, 아주머니	

B POINT를 참고하여 둘 중 알맞은 것을 골라 빈칸에 넣어 부정문을 완성하세요.

POINT

- It **was not** rainy yesterday.
- They **weren't** in the classroom.

be동사 과거형의 부정문은 was와 were 뒤에 not을 써서 만든다.
was not은 wasn't로, were not은 weren't로 줄여 쓴다.

1. I __________ tired yesterday. ☐ am not ☐ was not
2. She __________ in New York in 2000. ☐ isn't ☐ wasn't
3. My dad __________ a cook. ☐ was not ☐ were not
4. The children __________ in the park. ☐ wasn't ☐ weren't
5. She __________ our science teacher. ☐ wasn't ☐ weren't
6. They __________ in the same class. ☐ was not ☐ were not
7. He __________ at home last night. ☐ wasn't ☐ weren't
8. The cats __________ on the cat tower. ☐ wasn't ☐ weren't

C POINT를 참고하여 빈칸에 알맞은 be동사의 과거형을 써 넣어 의문문을 완성하세요.

POINT

be동사 과거형의 의문문은 Was/Were를 주어 앞에 써서 만든다.

- **Was** it cold last weekend? 주어가 I, he, she, it, 단수 명사일 때는 was를 쓴다.
- **Were** you at the concert? 주어가 you, we, they, 복수 명사일 때는 were를 쓴다.

1. __________ you okay?
2. __________ the water cold?
3. __________ it sunny that day?
4. __________ they happy?
5. __________ the box heavy?
6. __________ she a fifth grader in 2017?
7. __________ they late for the party?
8. __________ your mother in the living room?

D POINT를 참고하여 질문에 알맞은 대답을 완성하세요.

POINT

- A: Were you angry about that?
  B: **Yes, I was. / No, I wasn't.**

be동사 과거형 의문문의 대답은 긍정이면 Yes, 부정이면 No로 한다.

1. A: Was he in the library after school? 그는 방과 후에 도서관에 있었니?
   B: No, ______________.
2. A: Were you sleepy this morning? 너는 오늘 아침에 졸렸니?
   B: Yes, ______________.
3. A: Were they students of this school? 그들은 이 학교의 학생들이었니?
   B: No, ______________.
4. A: Was Emily's coat black? 에밀리의 코트는 검은색이었니?
   B: Yes, ______________.

E 우리말 뜻을 참고하여 밑줄 친 부분을 바르게 고치세요.

1. You not were a bad child. → ______________
   너는 나쁜 아이가 아니었다.
2. We was not in France last year. → ______________
   우리는 작년에 프랑스에 있지 않았다.
3. The girls wasn't late for school. → ______________
   그 여자아이들은 학교에 늦지 않았다.
4. She weren't alone in the restaurant. → ______________
   그녀는 그 식당에 혼자 있지 않았다.
5. Is it cold yesterday? → ______________
   어제 날이 추웠나요?
6. Were the exam difficult? → ______________
   그 시험은 어려웠니?
7. Was the chocolate cookies sweet? → ______________
   그 초콜릿 쿠키는 달았니?

Challenge!

F

주어진 단어들과 알맞은 be동사를 사용하여 우리말과 같은 뜻의 영어 문장을 쓰세요. (필요한 단어들을 추가하세요.)

1. 그는 유명한 피아니스트가 아니었다. (a famous pianist)

→ ______________________________

2. 그 새는 지붕 위에 있었나요? (the bird, on the roof)

→ ______________________________

3. 그들은 그때 학교에 없었다. (at school, at that time)

→ ______________________________

4. 어젯밤에 달이 밝았나요? (the moon, bright, last night)

→ ______________________________

5. 서울은 어제 흐리지 않았다. (it, cloudy, in Seoul, yesterday)

→ ______________________________

6. 그 가수의 목소리는 아름다웠나요? (the singer's voice, beautiful)

→ ______________________________

7. 우리는 그해에 같은 반이 아니었다. (in the same class, that year)

→ ______________________________

8. 그들은 지난 토요일에 집에 있었나요? (at home, last Saturday)

→ ______________________________

9. 그들은 그때 중학생이 아니었다. (middle school students, then)

→ ______________________________

10. 당신은 작년에 미국에 있었나요? (in the United States, last year)

→ ______________________________

UNIT 1 일반동사의 과거형 (규칙 변화)

A 다음 영어 단어에는 우리말 뜻을 쓰고, 우리말 뜻에는 영어 단어를 쓰세요.

	단어	우리말 뜻		우리말 뜻	단어
1	arrive		16	걱정하다	
2	be born		17	일하다	
3	dance		18	걷다	
4	design		19	시도하다, 노력하다	
5	drop		20	계획하다	
6	dry		21	열다	
7	enjoy		22	살다	
8	island		23	섬	
9	live		24	즐기다, 맛있게 먹다	
10	open		25	말리다, 건조시키다	
11	plan		26	떨어뜨리다	
12	try		27	설계하다, 디자인하다	
13	walk		28	춤추다	
14	work		29	태어나다	
15	worry		30	도착하다	

B POINT를 참고하여 주어진 동사의 알맞은 형태를 빈칸에 쓰세요.

POINT

과거에 했던 일이나 과거의 상태는 일반동사의 과거형으로 나타낸다. 과거에 '~했다'라는 뜻이다.

- I **played** the piano every day. 대부분의 동사는 동사원형에 -ed를 붙인다.
- They **lived** in Daejeon. -e로 끝나는 동사는 동사원형에 -d를 붙인다.
- She **studied** math last night. <자음+-y>로 끝나는 동사는 y를 i로 바꾸고 -ed를 붙인다.
- He **planned** a trip to Italy. <모음 1+자음 1>로 끝나는 동사는 자음을 한 번 더 쓰고 -ed를 붙인다.

1. I ______________ the bedroom window. (open) 나는 침실 창을 열었다.
2. We ______________ Chinese in 2020. (learn) 우리는 2020년에 중국어를 배웠다.
3. He ______________ the singer last year. (like) 그는 작년에 그 가수를 좋아했다.
4. The child ______________ last night. (cry) 그 아이는 어젯밤에 울었다.
5. The girl ______________ the glass then. (drop) 그 여자아이는 그때 유리잔을 떨어뜨렸다.

C POINT를 참고하여 우리말과 같은 뜻이 되도록 괄호 안에서 알맞은 것을 고르세요.

POINT

- I **play** soccer after school. 동사의 현재형은 현재 반복적으로 하는 일, 현재의 상태나 사실을 나타낸다.
- I **played** soccer yesterday. 동사의 과거형은 과거에 했던 일, 과거의 상태나 사실을 나타낸다.

1. 나는 피자를 좋아했다.
   → I (like / liked) pizza.
2. 그는 매일 1시간씩 걷는다.
   → He (walks / walked) for an hour every day.
3. 그들은 작년에 제주도로 이사했다.
   → They (move / moved) to Jeju Island last year.
4. 그 여자아이는 초콜릿 아이스크림을 원한다.
   → The girl (wants / wanted) chocolate ice cream.
5. 나는 어제 친구들과 야구를 했다.
   → I (play / played) baseball with my friends yesterday.

D 우리말과 같은 뜻이 되도록 빈칸에 알맞은 동사를 알맞은 형태로 쓰세요.

1. 우리 아빠는 동물원에서 일하셨다.
   → My dad ________________ at a zoo.

2. 나는 그 노래를 자주 들었다.
   → I often ________________ to the song.

3. 그는 오늘 아침에 자기 방을 청소했다.
   → He ________________ his room this morning.

4. 우리는 어제 도서관에서 공부했다.
   → We ________________ at the library yesterday.

5. 그들은 수학 시험에 대해 이야기했다.
   → They ________________ about their math exam.

6. 그녀는 거실 창문을 닫았다.
   → She ________________ the living room window.

E 우리말 뜻을 참고하여 밑줄 친 부분을 바르게 고치세요.

1. I wash my hair last night. → ________________
   나는 어젯밤에 머리를 감았다.

2. She helps an old man this morning. → ________________
   그녀는 오늘 아침에 할아버지 한 분을 도와드렸다.

3. Phil played basketball these days. → ________________
   필은 요즘 농구를 한다.

4. We watch a movie last weekend. → ________________
   우리는 지난 주말에 영화를 한 편 보았다.

5. My mom bakes cookies yesterday. → ________________
   우리 엄마가 어제 쿠키를 구우셨다.

6. They lived in the country now. → ________________
   그들은 지금 시골에 산다.

7. I plan a trip to America last year. → ________________
   나는 작년에 미국 여행을 계획했다.

Challenge!

F 주어진 단어들을 사용하여 우리말과 같은 뜻의 과거형 영어 문장을 쓰세요. (동사는 알맞은 형태로 바꾸고, 필요한 단어들을 추가하세요.)

1. 나는 창밖을 내다보았다. (look out, the window)

→ ______________________________

2. 그녀는 작년에 스페인어를 배웠다. (learn, Spanish, last year)

→ ______________________________

3. 그는 저녁으로 스테이크를 요리했다. (cook, steak, for dinner)

→ ______________________________

4. 그들은 지난 일요일에 축구를 했다. (play, soccer, last Sunday)

→ ______________________________

5. 그녀는 어젯밤에 한국사를 공부했다. (study, Korean history, last)

→ ______________________________

6. 우리는 30분 동안 그녀를 기다렸다. (wait for, for 30 minutes)

→ ______________________________

7. 나는 그때 록 음악을 무척 좋아했다. (rock music, very much, then)

→ ______________________________

8. 제임스는 10시 반에 역에 도착했다. (James, arrive, at the station, at)

→ ______________________________

9. 우리는 그 영화를 아주 재미있게 보았다. (enjoy, the movie, very much)

→ ______________________________

10. 그 아이는 저녁 식사 후에 양치질을 했다. (the child, brush, his teeth, after)

→ ______________________________

UNIT 2 일반동사의 과거형 (불규칙 변화)

A 다음 영어 단어에는 우리말 뜻을 쓰고, 우리말 뜻에는 영어 단어를 쓰세요.

	단어	우리말 뜻		우리말 뜻	단어
1	birthday		16	지갑	
2	favorite		17	말하다	
3	feel		18	놓다	
4	find		19	팔다	
5	hear		20	고기	
6	history		21	잃어버리다	
7	hit		22	알다	
8	hurt		23	다치게 하다	
9	know		24	치다	
10	lose		25	역사	
11	meat		26	듣다	
12	sell		27	찾다	
13	set		28	느끼다	
14	speak		29	특히 좋아하는	
15	wallet		30	생일	

B POINT를 참고하여 우리말 뜻에 맞게 주어진 동사의 과거형을 빈칸에 쓰세요.

POINT

- She **went** to school at 8. I **met** Jimmy on the street.

현재형과 과거형의 형태가 완전히 다른 동사들이 있다.

1. I ______________ a letter to him. (write) 나는 그에게 편지를 썼다.
2. She ______________ cereal for breakfast. (eat) 그녀는 아침으로 시리얼을 먹었다.
3. We ______________ a movie last Sunday. (see) 우리는 지난 일요일에 영화를 한 편 보았다.
4. Jennifer ______________ home at 7 p.m. (come) 제니퍼는 오후 일곱 시에 집에 왔다.
5. My mom ______________ a doll for me. (make) 엄마가 나에게 인형을 만들어주셨다.
6. He ______________ on the sofa last night. (sleep) 그는 어젯밤에 소파에서 잤다.
7. The man ______________ a shower after work. (take)
   그 남자는 일을 하고 나서 샤워를 했다.
8. I ______________ a glass of milk this morning. (drink)
   나는 오늘 아침에 우유를 한 잔 마셨다.
9. She ______________ English at a middle school. (teach)
   그녀는 중학교에서 영어를 가르쳤다.

C POINT를 참고하여 우리말 뜻에 맞게 주어진 동사의 과거형을 빈칸에 쓰세요.

POINT

- I **read** a book last night.

현재형과 과거형의 형태가 같은 동사들이 있다.

1. He ______________ a baseball with a bat. (hit) 그는 방망이로 야구공을 쳤다.
2. My mom ______________ the watermelon with a knife. (cut)
   우리 엄마는 칼로 수박을 자르셨다.
3. The girl ______________ a book called *Snow White*. (read)
   그 여자아이는 《백설공주》라는 책을 읽었다.
4. She ______________ a picture of her dog on the desk. (put)
   그녀는 책상 위에 자신의 강아지 사진을 놔두었다.

D 우리말과 같은 뜻이 되도록 빈칸에 알맞은 동사를 알맞은 형태로 쓰세요.

1. 나는 빨간색 스웨터를 갖고 있었다.
   → I ______________ a red sweater.

2. 그녀는 새 지갑을 하나 샀다.
   → She ______________ a new purse.

3. 소미는 오늘 5시에 집에 왔다.
   → Somi ______________ home at 5 today.

4. 우리는 작년에 런던에 갔다.
   → We ______________ to London last year.

5. 그는 그 여자아이에게 곰 인형을 주었다.
   → He ______________ a teddy bear to the girl.

6. 과학 수업은 9시에 시작되었다.
   → Science class ______________ at 9 o'clock.

E 우리말 뜻을 참고하여 밑줄 친 부분을 바르게 고치세요.

1. He putted the glass down on the table. → ______________
   그는 탁자에 유리잔을 내려놓았다.

2. The girl run for 30 minutes yesterday. → ______________
   그 여자아이는 어제 30분 동안 달렸다.

3. I getted up at 7 this morning. → ______________
   나는 오늘 아침 7시에 일어났다.

4. They sell vegetables at the store then. → ______________
   그 가게에서는 그때 채소를 팔았다.

5. We meet her at the station last night. → ______________
   우리는 어젯밤 역에서 그녀를 만났다.

6. She teached third graders last year. → ______________
   그녀는 작년에 3학년 학생들을 가르쳤다.

Challenge!

F

주어진 단어들을 사용하여 우리말과 같은 뜻의 과거형 영어 문장을 쓰세요. (동사는 알맞은 형태로 바꾸고, 필요한 단어들을 추가하세요.)

1. 그는 어제 10시간 동안 잤다. (sleep, for 10 hours)

→ ______________________________

2. 나는 오늘 옥수수수프를 만들었다. (make, corn soup)

→ ______________________________

3. 앤디가 나에게 그 책을 주었다. (Andy, give, the book, to me)

→ ______________________________

4. 그는 미나의 전화번호를 알았다. (know, Mina's, phone number)

→ ______________________________

5. 그 아이들은 크리스마스 캐럴을 불렀다. (sing, Christmas carols)

→ ______________________________

6. 그녀가 나에게 웃긴 이야기를 하나 해주었다. (tell, me, a funny story)

→ ______________________________

7. 그는 저녁을 먹기 전에 숙제를 했다. (his homework, before dinner)

→ ______________________________

8. 그녀는 회색 고양이 그림을 그렸다. (draw, a picture of, a gray cat)

→ ______________________________

9. 나는 점심으로 달걀 샌드위치를 먹었다. (eat, an egg sandwich, for)

→ ______________________________

10. 데이비드는 그에 관한 소식을 들었다. (David, hear, the news, about)

→ ______________________________

UNIT 3 일반동사 과거형의 부정문, 의문문

A 다음 영어 단어에는 우리말 뜻을 쓰고, 우리말 뜻에는 영어 단어를 쓰세요.

	단어	우리말 뜻		우리말 뜻	단어
1	begin		16	여행하다	
2	buy		17	점수	
3	drive		18	그림	
4	fall		19	소풍	
5	finish		20	국수	
6	homework		21	만나다	
7	kitchen		22	식사	
8	marathon		23	마라톤	
9	meal		24	주방, 부엌	
10	meet		25	숙제	
11	noodle		26	끝마치다	
12	picnic		27	가을	
13	picture		28	운전하다	
14	score		29	사다	
15	travel		30	시작하다, 시작되다	

B POINT를 참고하여 주어진 동사를 사용하여 과거형 부정문을 완성하세요.

POINT
- She **did not have** breakfast this morning.

과거에 '~하지 않았다'라는 뜻의 일반동사 과거형의 부정문은 did not을 동사원형 앞에 쓴다.

- She **didn't have** breakfast this morning. did not은 didn't로 줄여 쓸 수 있다.

1. It ____________ yesterday. (rain) 어제는 비가 오지 않았다.
2. Joseph ____________ last night. (sleep) 조셉은 어젯밤에 잠을 자지 않았다.
3. I ____________ for a walk yesterday. (go) 나는 어제 산책을 가지 않았다.
4. Annie ____________ the hamburger. (eat) 애니는 그 햄버거를 먹지 않았다.
5. He ____________ TV last weekend. (watch) 그는 지난 주말에 TV를 보지 않았다.
6. They ____________ in LA at that time. (live) 그들은 그때 LA에 살지 않았다.
7. I ____________ the bus this morning. (take) 나는 오늘 아침에 버스를 타지 않았다.

C POINT를 참고하여 주어진 주어와 동사를 사용하여 과거형 의문문을 완성하세요.

POINT
- **Did** you **have** breakfast this morning?

과거에 '~했나요?'라고 묻는 일반동사 과거형의 의문문은 did를 문장 맨 앞에 써서 <Did+주어+동사원형 ~?>으로 한다.

1. ____________ his hands? (he, wash) 그가 손을 닦았나요?
2. ____________ to the movies? (she, go) 그녀가 영화를 보러 갔나요?
3. ____________ your homework? (you, finish) 너 숙제 다 끝냈니?
4. ____________ the window of the room? (you, close) 너 그 방 창문 닫았어?
5. ____________ music at the school? (Mr. Smith, teach)
스미스 씨가 그 학교에서 음악을 가르쳤나요?
6. ____________ basketball after school? (the boys, play)
그 남자아이들은 수업이 끝나고 농구를 했나요?
7. ____________ letters to their parents? (the children, write)
그 아이들은 부모님께 편지를 썼나요?

D POINT를 참고하여 질문에 대한 대답을 완성하세요.

POINT

- A: Did you meet Katie yesterday?
  B: **Yes, I did.** / **No, I didn't.**

일반동사 과거형 의문문의 대답은 긍정이면 Yes, 부정이면 No로 한다.

1. A: Did you sleep well last night? 어젯밤에 잘 잤어요?
   B: Yes, ______________.
2. A: Did Sarah make this pasta? 사라가 이 파스타를 만들었어요?
   B: No, ______________.
3. A: Did you read his new book? 너 그의 새 책 읽었어?
   B: No, ______________.
4. A: Did they go on a picnic last Saturday? 그들은 지난 토요일에 소풍을 갔나요?
   B: No, ______________.

E 우리말 뜻을 참고하여 틀린 부분을 찾아 바르게 고치세요.

1. I studied not in the library yesterday. 나는 어제 도서관에서 공부하지 않았다.
   ______________ → ______________
2. Did you took a shower this morning? 너 오늘 아침에 샤워했어?
   ______________ → ______________
3. We didn't visited the museum in 2020. 우리는 2020년에 그 박물관을 방문하지 않았다.
   ______________ → ______________
4. Did she does the dishes after dinner? 그녀가 저녁 식사 후에 설거지를 했나요?
   ______________ → ______________
5. He didn't not clean the house today. 그는 오늘 집을 청소하지 않았다.
   ______________ → ______________

Challenge!

F 주어진 단어들을 사용하여 우리말과 같은 뜻의 과거형 영어 문장을 쓰세요. (동사는 알맞은 형태로 바꾸고, 필요한 단어들을 추가하세요.)

1. 그는 평일에는 요리를 하지 않았다. (cook, on weekdays)

→ ______________________________

2. 너는 집에서 점심을 먹었니? (have lunch, at home)

→ ______________________________

3. 나는 그날 모자를 쓰지 않았다. (wear a cap, that day)

→ ______________________________

4. 피터는 버스로 학교에 왔나요? (Peter, come, to school, by bus)

→ ______________________________

5. 그는 그때 중학교에 다니지 않았다. (go, to middle school, then)

→ ______________________________

6. 그들은 지난 토요일에 그녀를 방문했나요? (visit, her, last Saturday)

→ ______________________________

7. 나는 오늘 아침 6시에 일어나지 않았다. (get up, at, this morning)

→ ______________________________

8. 너는 지난 일요일에 꽃 축제에 갔니? (go, to the flower festival, last)

→ ______________________________

9. 나는 그 당시에 팟캐스트를 듣지 않았다. (listen, to podcasts, at the time)

→ ______________________________

10. 제니퍼는 작년에 발레를 배웠나요? (Jennifer, learn, ballet, last year)

→ ______________________________

UNIT 1 부사의 형태와 쓰임

A 다음 영어 단어에는 우리말 뜻을 쓰고, 우리말 뜻에는 영어 단어를 쓰세요.

	단어	우리말 뜻		우리말 뜻	단어
1	athlete		16	잘	
2	carefully		17	웃다, 미소 짓다	
3	diligent		18	천천히, 느리게	
4	early		19	안전한	
5	hard		20	정말로	
6	hospital		21	조용히	
7	low		22	빨리, 신속하게	
8	puppy		23	강아지	
9	quickly		24	낮은; 낮게	
10	quietly		25	병원	
11	really		26	힘든, 어려운; 열심히	
12	safe		27	이른, 일찍	
13	slowly		28	성실한, 근면한	
14	smile		29	조심스럽게, 주의 깊게	
15	well		30	운동선수, 육상선수	

B POINT를 참고하여 각 문장에서 부사를 찾아 빈칸에 쓰세요.

POINT
- We went to the zoo **yesterday**. 부사는 때를 나타낸다.
- She came **here** by bus. 부사는 장소를 나타낸다.
- Horses run **fast**. 부사는 방법이나 정도를 나타낸다.

1. That old man walks slowly. ______________
   저 노인은 천천히 걷는다.
2. The mountain is very high. ______________
   그 산은 매우 높다.
3. This is a really funny movie. ______________
   이것은 정말 웃긴 영화다.
4. I saw Emily on the street today. ______________
   나는 오늘 거리에서 에밀리를 보았다.

C POINT를 참고하여 각 문장에서 부사와 그 부사가 꾸미는 단어를 찾아 쓰세요.

POINT
- Jimmy **came** to the station late. 부사는 동사를 꾸민다.
- Sarah is very **smart**. 부사는 형용사를 꾸민다.
- The girl dances really **well**. 부사는 다른 부사를 꾸민다.

1. The girl plays badminton well. 그 여자아이는 배드민턴을 잘 친다.
   부사 : ______________ 부사가 꾸미는 단어 : ______________
2. This book is really interesting. 이 책은 정말 재미있다.
   부사 : ______________ 부사가 꾸미는 단어 : ______________
3. He solves math problems very easily. 그는 수학 문제를 아주 쉽게 푼다.
   부사 : ______________ 부사가 꾸미는 단어 : ______________
4. She left for Iceland yesterday. 그녀는 어제 아이슬란드로 떠났다.
   부사 : ______________ 부사가 꾸미는 단어 : ______________

D POINT를 참고하여 주어진 형용사를 부사로 바꾸어 빈칸에 쓰세요.

POINT

- He speaks **kindly** to people. 대부분의 부사가 형용사에 -ly를 붙인 형태다.
- They live **happily** in the house. I **simply** don't want it.
  -y로 끝나는 형용사는 y를 지우고 -ily를 붙이고, -le로 끝나는 형용사는 e를 빼고 -y를 붙인다.
- She goes to school **early**. 형용사와 부사의 형태가 같은 것들도 있다.

1. She ______________ closed her eyes. (gentle)
   그녀는 살며시 눈을 감았다.

2. The man ______________ ran away. (quick)
   그 남자는 재빨리 도망쳤다.

3. Jake arrived at the station ______________. (early)
   제이크는 역에 일찍 도착했다.

4. The boy called his mother ______________. (loud)
   그 남자아이는 큰 소리로 엄마를 불렀다.

5. We can ______________ get to his house from here. (easy)
   우리는 여기서 그의 집에 쉽게 갈 수 있다.

6. She listened ______________ to her teacher during class. (careful)
   그녀는 수업 시간에 선생님 말씀을 주의 깊게 들었다.

E 우리말 뜻을 참고하여 밑줄 친 부분을 바르게 고치세요.

1. Youngmin studies English hardly. → ______________
   영민이는 영어를 열심히 공부한다.

2. My dad speaks Chinese good. → ______________
   우리 아빠는 중국어를 잘하신다.

3. They are smiling happyly together. → ______________
   그들은 함께 행복하게 미소 짓고 있다.

4. This soup is delicious really. → ______________
   이 수프는 정말 맛있다.

5. The boy got up lately this morning. → ______________
   그 남자아이는 오늘 아침에 늦게 일어났다.

Challenge!

F 주어진 단어들을 사용하여 우리말과 같은 뜻의 영어 문장을 쓰세요. (동사는 알맞은 형태로 바꾸고, 필요한 단어들을 추가하세요.)

1. 나의 방은 정말 작다. (my, really, small)

→ ______________________________

2. 그는 제이미를 잘 안다. (know, Jamie, well)

→ ______________________________

3. 그 정원은 매우 아름답다. (the garden, very)

→ ______________________________

4. 그 새는 높이 날고 있다. (the bird, fly, high)

→ ______________________________

5. 그녀는 그의 말을 주의 깊게 들었다. (listen, to him, carefully)

→ ______________________________

6. 그 사람은 2020년에 여기서 일했다. (the man, work, here, in)

→ ______________________________

7. 그 가족은 일찍 잠자리에 들었다. (the family, go to bed, early)

→ ______________________________

8. 그녀는 그 노인에게 천천히 말했다. (speak, slowly, to the old man)

→ ______________________________

9. 크리스는 시험공부를 열심히 했다. (Chris, hard, for the exam)

→ ______________________________

10. 그는 아기를 보고 다정하게 웃었다. (smile, gently, at the baby)

→ ______________________________

UNIT 2 빈도부사

다음 영어 단어에는 우리말 뜻을 쓰고, 우리말 뜻에는 영어 단어를 쓰세요.

	단어	우리말 뜻		우리말 뜻	단어
1	alone		16	보통, 대개	
2	always		17	여행	
3	appointment		18	때때로, 가끔	
4	climb		19	자주	
5	customer		20	시끄러운	
6	forget		21	절대 ~ 않는	
7	friendly		22	산	
8	hobby		23	취미	
9	mountain		24	친절한, 상냥한	
10	never		25	잊어버리다	
11	noisy		26	손님, 고객	
12	often		27	오르다	
13	sometimes		28	(만날) 약속	
14	trip		29	항상, 언제나	
15	usually		30	혼자	

B POINT를 참고하여 각 문장에서 빈도부사를 골라 빈칸에 쓰세요.

POINT

- She **usually** arrives at school at 8 a.m.

빈도부사는 어떤 행동을 얼마나 자주 하는지, 어떤 일이 얼마나 자주 일어나는지를 나타내는 부사로, always(항상), usually(보통, 대개), often(자주), sometimes(때때로, 가끔), never(절대 ~ 않는) 등이 있다.

1. It often rains in this area. ____________
   이 지역은 비가 자주 온다.
2. I never went to bed after 10 p.m. ____________
   나는 밤 10시 넘어서 잠자리에 든 적이 없다.
3. They always watch TV after dinner. ____________
   그들은 항상 저녁 식사 후에 TV를 본다.
4. He sometimes goes to the library after school. ____________
   그는 가끔 방과 후에 도서관에 간다.
5. She usually goes camping with her family on weekends. ____________
   그녀는 주말에는 보통 가족들과 캠핑을 간다.

C POINT를 참고하여 주어진 빈도부사가 들어갈 자리에 √ 표시 하세요.

POINT

- He **is always** kind to others. | 빈도부사는 be동사와 조동사 뒤에 온다.
- She **always eats** dinner at home. | 빈도부사는 일반동사 앞에 온다.

1. never — Paul is late for school.
2. never — Paul eats cucumbers.
3. usually — I am at home on Sundays.
4. often — I exercise in the evening.
5. sometimes — She goes shopping alone.
6. sometimes — She may play mobile games.

D 우리말과 같은 뜻이 되도록 빈칸에 알맞은 빈도부사를 쓰세요.

1. 나는 항상 식사 후에 양치질을 한다.
   → I ______________ brush my teeth after meals.

2. 우리는 가끔 주말에 등산을 간다.
   → We ______________ go hiking on weekends.

3. 그는 절대로 자기 방 청소를 하지 않는다.
   → He ______________ cleans his room.

4. 그들은 자주 패스트푸드 식당에 간다.
   → They ______________ go to fast-food restaurants.

5. 그녀는 보통 아침에 30분씩 달리기를 한다.
   → She ______________ runs for 30 minutes in the morning.

6. 내 고양이는 가끔 내 무릎에서 잔다.
   → My cat ______________ sleeps on my lap.

E 우리말 뜻을 참고하여 틀린 부분을 바르게 고쳐 문장을 다시 쓰세요.

1. They eat out never. 그들은 외식을 전혀 하지 않는다.
   → ______________________________

2. Joy always is cheerful. 조이는 항상 명랑하다.
   → ______________________________

3 He goes usually to school by bike. 그는 보통 자전거를 타고 학교에 간다.
   → ______________________________

4. She drinks often hot chocolate in winter. 그녀는 겨울에 자주 핫초콜릿을 마신다.
   → ______________________________

5. You always should wash your hands before meals.
   식사를 하기 전에는 항상 손을 씻어야 한다.
   → ______________________________

Challenge!

F 주어진 단어들과 알맞은 빈도부사를 사용하여 우리말과 같은 뜻의 영어 문장을 쓰세요. (동사는 알맞은 형태로 바꾸고, 필요한 단어들을 추가하세요.)

1. 그들은 보드게임을 자주 한다. (play, board games)

→ ______________________________

2. 그는 절대 찬물을 마시지 않는다. (drink, cold water)

→ ______________________________

3. 우리 아빠는 자주 파스타를 만드신다. (my dad, make, pasta)

→ ______________________________

4. 대니얼은 가끔 회사에 늦는다. (Daniel, late, for work)

→ ______________________________

5. 너는 가끔 아이스크림을 먹어도 된다. (may, eat, ice cream)

→ ______________________________

6. 그는 보통 오후 7시에 귀가한다. (come back home, at 7 p.m.)

→ ______________________________

7. 나는 아침에 항상 수프를 먹는다. (soup, in the morning)

→ ______________________________

8. 그 사람은 신문을 전혀 읽지 않는다. (the man, read, newspapers)

→ ______________________________

9. 우리 엄마는 보통 버스로 출근하신다. (mom, go to work, by bus)

→ ______________________________

10. 너는 비 오는 날은 항상 창을 닫아야 한다. (should, close the window, on rainy days)

→ ______________________________

UNIT 1 시간의 전치사

A 다음 영어 단어에는 우리말 뜻을 쓰고, 우리말 뜻에는 영어 단어를 쓰세요.

	단어	우리말 뜻		우리말 뜻	단어
1	August		16	화요일	
2	bloom		17	해넘이, 일몰	
3	December		18	해돋이, 일출	
4	humid		19	간식	
5	January		20	9월	
6	March		21	연습하다	
7	midnight		22	11월	
8	noon		23	정오, 낮 12시	
9	November		24	자정, 밤 12시	
10	practice		25	3월	
11	September		26	1월	
12	snack		27	습한	
13	sunrise		28	12월	
14	sunset		29	꽃이 피다	
15	Tuesday		30	8월	

B POINT를 참고하여 빈칸에 at, on, in 중 알맞은 전치사를 쓰세요.

POINT
- I got up **at 7** this morning. | 시간, 정오(noon), 밤(night), 자정(midnight) 앞에는 전치사 at을 쓴다.
- He watches movies **on Sundays.** | 날짜, 요일, 특정한 날 앞에는 전치사 on을 쓴다.
- We moved here **in 2020.** | 월, 계절, 연도, 아침, 오후, 저녁 앞에는 전치사 in을 쓴다.

1. I take piano lessons ________ Mondays. 나는 월요일에 피아노 강습을 받는다.
2. The department store opens ________ 10 a.m. 그 백화점은 오전 10시에 문을 연다.
3. She entered elementary school ________ 2015. 그녀는 2015년에 초등학교에 들어갔다.
4. They watched the sunrise ________ New Year's Day. 그들은 새해 첫날에 해돋이를 보았다.
5. He often goes camping ________ spring and autumn. 그는 봄과 가을에 자주 캠핑을 간다.
6. You must not go out alone ________ night. 너는 밤에 혼자 밖에 나가면 안 된다.
7. The autumn leaves are beautiful ________ November. 11월에는 단풍이 아름답다.

C POINT를 참고하여 우리말 뜻에 맞게 빈칸에 before, after, for 중 알맞은 전치사를 쓰세요.

POINT
- Wash your hands **before dinner.** | before는 '~ 전에'라는 뜻의 전치사다.
- They play soccer **after school.** | after는 '~ 후에/뒤에/다음에'라는 뜻의 전치사다.
- She exercises **for an hour.** | for는 '~ 동안'이라는 뜻의 전치사다.

1. Let's play badminton ________ class. 수업 끝나고 배드민턴 치자.
2. My grandmother gets up ________ sunrise. 우리 할머니는 해 뜨기 전에 일어나신다.
3. I read books ________ an hour every day. 나는 매일 1시간 동안 책을 읽는다.
4. She doesn't eat anything ________ 7 p.m. 그녀는 저녁 7시 이후에 아무것도 먹지 않는다.
5. They traveled in Europe ________ two months. 그들은 두 달 동안 유럽을 여행했다.
6. The singer drank water ________ the concert. 그 가수는 공연 전에 물을 마셨다.
7. We took pictures ________ the party. 우리는 파티가 끝난 후에 사진을 찍었다.
8. My dad didn't wash his car ________ a year. 우리 아빠는 1년 동안 세차하지 않으셨다.

D 우리말과 같은 뜻이 되도록 빈칸에 알맞은 전치사를 쓰세요.

1. 그 기차는 정오에 서울로 출발했다.
   → The train left for Seoul ________ noon.

2. 그녀는 한 달 동안 그 섬에 살았다.
   → She lived on the island ________ a month.

3. 나는 8시 전에 그에게 전화를 해야 한다.
   → I have to call him ________ 8 o'clock.

4. 나는 5시 30분에 극장 앞에서 그녀를 만났다.
   → I met her in front of the theater ________ 5:30.

5. 에밀리는 저녁을 먹고 나서 일기를 쓴다.
   → Emily writes in her diary ________ dinner.

6. 그는 생일에 선물을 많이 받았다.
   → He received a lot of gifts ________ his birthday.

7. 그녀는 보통 오후에 강아지와 산책을 한다.
   → She usually takes a walk with her dog ________ the afternoon.

E 우리말 뜻을 참고하여 밑줄 친 부분을 바르게 고치세요.

1. I first went to the city at 2018. → ________
   나는 2018년에 그 도시에 처음 갔다.

2. It snows often here on winter. → ________
   겨울에 이곳에는 눈이 자주 온다.

3. The lights go out before midnight. → ________
   자정 이후에는 전등이 꺼진다.

4. Their concert is in December 24th. → ________
   그들의 콘서트는 12월 24일에 열린다.

5. I have to do my homework after 9 o'clock. → ________
   나는 9시 전에 숙제를 해야 한다.

Challenge!

F 주어진 단어들과 알맞은 전치사를 사용하여 우리말과 같은 뜻의 영어 문장을 쓰세요. (동사는 알맞은 형태로 바꾸고, 필요한 단어들을 추가하세요.)

1. 그는 저녁에 숙제를 한다. (do, his homework)

→ ______________________________

2. 그들은 50분 동안 축구를 했다. (play, soccer, 50 minutes)

→ ______________________________

3. 그 영화는 오전 11시에 시작했다. (the movie, begin, 11 a.m.)

→ ______________________________

4. 우리 아빠는 일요일에 낚시를 가신다. (my dad, go, fishing, Sundays)

→ ______________________________

5. 그녀는 늘 저녁 식사 후에 산책을 한다. (always, take, a walk, dinner)

→ ______________________________

6. 나는 여름에 아이스크림을 많이 먹는다. (eat, a lot of ice cream, summer)

→ ______________________________

7. 그녀는 5월 12일에 뉴욕에 갔다. (go, to New York, May 12th)

→ ______________________________

8. 우리는 영어 수업 전에 수학 수업이 있다. (have, math class, English class)

→ ______________________________

9. 그들은 수업이 끝난 후에 자주 만화책을 읽었다. (often, read, comic books, school)

→ ______________________________

10. 학생들과 교사들은 정오에 점심을 먹는다. (the students and teachers, have, lunch)

→ ______________________________

UNIT 2 위치, 장소의 전치사

A 다음 영어 단어에는 우리말 뜻을 쓰고, 우리말 뜻에는 영어 단어를 쓰세요.

	단어	우리말 뜻		우리말 뜻	단어
1	bank		16	가게, 상점	
2	behind		17	서 있다	
3	beside		18	경기장	
4	between		19	강	
5	bookshelf		20	~ 가까이에	
6	building		21	미술관, 화랑	
7	cinema		22	백화점	
8	college		23	대학(교)	
9	department store		24	영화관	
10	gallery		25	건물	
11	near		26	책꽂이, 책장	
12	river		27	사이에	
13	stadium		28	~ 옆에	
14	stand		29	~ 뒤에	
15	store		30	은행	

B POINT를 참고하여 우리말 뜻에 맞게 괄호 안에서 알맞은 전치사를 고르세요.

POINT

- The cat is **in** the box. The bird is **on** the roof.
  The dog is **under** the table. My house is **behind** the college.

위치를 나타내는 전치사들에는 in(~ 안에), on(~ 위에), under(~ 아래에), near(~ 가까이에), in front of(~ 앞에), behind(~ 뒤에), next to/beside(~ 옆에), between A and B(A와 B 사이에) 등이 있다.

1. 고양이 한 마리가 피아노 위에 있다.
   → A cat is (on / under) the piano.
2. 민호는 지민이 뒤에 앉아 있다.
   → Minho is sitting (between / behind) Jimin.
3. 우리 학교 근처에 경기장이 있다.
   → There is a stadium (next to / near) my school.
4. 그의 책가방은 책상 밑에 있었다.
   → His schoolbag was (in / under) the desk.
5. 그 집 앞에 자동차가 한 대 있다.
   → There is a car (in front of / behind) the house.

C POINT를 참고하여 우리말 뜻에 맞게 괄호 안에서 알맞은 전치사를 고르세요.

POINT

- They live **in** Hong Kong. in은 비교적 넓은 장소 앞에서 '~에서'라는 뜻을 나타낸다.
- I met her **at** the bus stop. at은 비교적 좁은 장소 앞에서 '~에서'라는 뜻을 나타낸다.

1. 나는 춘천에서 자랐다.
   → I grew up (at / in) Chuncheon.
2. 우리는 집에서 크리스마스 파티를 했다.
   → We had a Christmas party (at / in) home.
3. 그녀는 아일랜드에서 간호사로 일했다.
   → She worked as a nurse (at / in) Ireland.

D 우리말과 같은 뜻이 되도록 빈칸에 알맞은 전치사를 쓰세요.

1. 스웨덴은 노르웨이 옆에 있다.
   → Sweden is ____________ to Norway.

2. 그 아이들은 학교에서 점심을 먹는다.
   → The children eat lunch ____________ school.

3. 그 아이는 모르는 사람들 앞에서는 조용하다.
   → The child is quiet ____________ of strangers.

4. 나는 극장에서 그 사람 뒤에 앉아 있었다.
   → I was sitting ____________ him in the theater.

5. 탁자 위에 책 두 권과 머그잔 하나가 있다.
   → There are two books and a mug ____________ the table.

6. 그의 집 근처에 공장이 몇 곳 있다.
   → There are several factories ____________ his house.

E 우리말 뜻을 참고하여 밑줄 친 부분을 바르게 고치세요.

1. I lived at that city last year. → ____________
   나는 작년에 그 도시에 살았다.

2. The museum is between the library. → ____________
   박물관은 도서관 뒤에 있다.

3. The man is standing next from the truck. → ____________
   그 남자는 트럭 옆에 서 있다.

4. There was a mailbox on the streetlamp. → ____________
   가로등 밑에 우체통이 있었다.

5. A woman is in front at the store. → ____________
   한 여성이 그 상점 앞에 있다.

6. There is a subway station next the park. → ____________
   그 공원 근처에 지하철역이 있다.

Challenge!

F 주어진 단어들과 알맞은 전치사를 사용하여 우리말과 같은 뜻의 영어 문장을 쓰세요. (동사는 알맞은 형태로 바꾸고, 필요한 단어들을 추가하세요.)

1. 우리 집은 공항 근처에 있다. (my house, the airport)

→ ______________________________

2. 그는 학교에서 숙제를 한다. (do, his homework)

→ ______________________________

3. 탁자 위에 달력이 있다. (there, a calendar, the table)

→ ______________________________

4. 그 병원은 우체국 옆에 있다. (the hospital, the post office)

→ ______________________________

5. 그 학교 뒤에 낮은 산이 있다. (there, a low hill, the school)

→ ______________________________

6. 리오와 나는 런던에서 처음 만났다. (Leo, first, meet, London)

→ ______________________________

7. 그의 안경은 책상 서랍 안에 있었다. (glasses, the desk drawer)

→ ______________________________

8. 지하철역이 그 대학교 앞에 있다. (a subway station, the college)

→ ______________________________

9. 그 가게는 빵집과 꽃집 사이에 있다. (the store, the bakery, the flower shop)

→ ______________________________

10. 그때는 그 나무 아래에 벤치가 있었다. (at that time, there, a bench, the tree)

→ ______________________________